Bishops

Bishops

MY TURBULENT COLONIAL YOUTH

Mona Williams

MALLINSON RENDEL

For Sarah, Adri, Rose, Zeyda and Helen

ACKNOWLEDGEMENTS

The author is deeply indebted to the Queen Elizabeth II Arts Council of New Zealand and the University of Waikato whose joint award of the 1993 Writer in Residence Fellowship afforded her the time to finish this book.

The author further acknowledges the generosity of the Palmerston North College of Education whose Council permitted her a year's leave of absence to write.

Mallinson Rendel Publishers gratefully acknowledge the assistance of the Children's Publication Fund which has made publication possible.

NOTE

Before Independence in 1966 the Republic of Guyana in South America was known as British Guiana.

First published in New Zealand by
Mallinson Rendel Publishers Ltd
P.O. Box 9409, Wellington

ISBN 908783-05-1
Typeset by Wright & Carman Ltd, Trentham
Printed by Colorcraft Ltd, Hong Kong

One

I am older than three but younger than four years old. Mummy and I are alone and Mummy stands me up against the door of my grandmother Mudsie's bedroom. The skin at the back of my head touches the slats in the door, as I have very little hair to braid into plaits. I bump my head very gently against the slats. Mummy stoops down and moves her face close, in front of my nose.

"Say what I tell you," she directs me. "Say, I will go to Bishops!" The words are teased out deliberately.

"I gun go to Bishops," I parrot imperfectly in Creolese.

Understanding neither the words I've said nor their importance, they are etched into my brain as I gently touch my head against the door slats repeatedly. Reflecting on this as I grow older, I see it clearly as the exact moment when my turbulent river journey began.

"Spell wool," Mr McGowan's voice said in an off-hand fashion. His Parker pen scored vivid red marks on my exercise book under his pudgy fist.

"W-o-l", I whispered, my attention somewhat unfocused, my gaze having travelled over the scene below me.

I was fascinated by my still strange school mates. The girls wore navy blue tunics and white cotton blouses, the boys khaki pants and white shirts. Most were barefoot. Mummy hadn't yet sent my uniform so I was wearing a delicate, organdie party blouse over a pink and white, ribbon and lace camisole. My skirt was made from floral material and my pink and white cotton socks were hand knitted. I wore black patent leather shoes. I caught a whiff of the talcum powder Mudsie had given me for the year and with which I had dusted, Yardley's Lavender.

The faintest murmur pervaded the school house from one hundred and fifty heads bent reading, counting, writing and chanting. Oiled and combed fleecy black mounds covered the heads of pupils of African descent. The girls, like me, had their hair parted into neat squares, plaited and held with ribbons. Straight, long, shiny black hair slicked with water topped the heads of the East Indian pupils.

"What!" the headmaster roared. I jumped. The school instantly hushed. All eyes shot towards the stage.

"W-u-l," I attempted, scenting danger, my full attention now on the headmaster.

"Whaaaat?" I would have heard him had he whispered, but he seemed intent on entertaining the school. His big frame pushed back the bent-wood chair with its woven cane seat. His right hand grasped the curved neck of his wild cane and his towering form lunged towards me. "What?" came the bellow.

"W-u-l," I tried. "W-o-l-l," I wavered.

"You're sitting scholarship and you can't spell wool!"

My eyes travelled from the white shirt collar to the square, newly shaved jowl. His nostrils were flared and his eyes terrifying. He raised his hand.

Jiggling with every wrist movement was his sixth finger, the length of one joint. The dangling 'wee bumblebee' of a finger transfixed me as a cobra would a toad. My brains felt scrambled, disorganised, like chopped up spaghetti. 'Whack! Whack!' He aimed the blows over my head and on to the back of my organdie blouse.

"Spell wool!" screamed Mr McGowan. "Spell wool!"

"W-o-l-e? . . . W-u-u-l?" I blurted.

"Whaaat?" roared the voice. 'Whack! Whack!' echoed the cane. There was no other sound from the entire school. Now the four other teachers stood staring at the cobra and the toad.

Mesmerised, facing the headmaster while backing away and descending the stairs, I seemed to be performing a strange dance. It reminded me of the movements of a coconut tree in a hurricane. His snake-jabs allowed the cane to flick easily at different angles across my lowering back. Besides, having stepped downwards, precisely where was there to go three rungs later? Desperation urged me to bolt but my escape was blocked by towering book cupboards and long desks.

"Eh! Eh!" my score-keeper mind commented. "That's six hard lashes for spelling just one word wrong!"

Plunging into the gap between two cupboards, I'd now exposed my back to the cane. The rain of lashes continued mightily to the accompanying bellow, "Spell wool!"

I gave up, and sensing that this was the required response let out a torrent of anguished screams. Magically, the hurricane ceased immediately. I had admitted to being broken, vanquished. Emerging from between the bookcases I faced Mr McGowan's back which now resembled that of a General in a war movie. He marched triumphantly up to the platform, picked up my book and flung it at me with mock rage. "And do your corrections!" All that over one spelling mistake? Regaining his seat he glared at the entire school. Swiftly one hundred and fifty heads bowed to their books. What was it that I saw? I looked again. Unlike other teachers, whose faces might have shown fury, Mr McGowan's held a barely suppressed smile of satisfaction.

Sliding into my seat a new terror swept over me. I realised that my brain still had no idea of how to spell this alien word. Wool was not part of our daily life in sweltering, equatorial, sea-level British Guiana, neither was this word. What's more, I read and wrote formal English but did not speak it outside

3

of the classroom. My mind argued angrily, "Each try at spelling gave the sound I was asked for. How else would you pronounce 'whole,wul,woll'?"

Sobbing, I reasoned, "If Mr McGowan was so anxious for me to spell correctly why didn't he show me how to guess or how to search for the answer. What is the good of being as ignorant after, as I was before the flogging? This moment is just as I'd read in one of my English books, 'Great cry and little wool'!"

"W-o-o-l," whispered Lucy, my desk-mate. That spelling made less sense then my "W-u-l." but having no choice I wrote it. Then, to make doubly sure, I looked up "WOOL" in the school's big *Shorter Oxford Dictionary*. Lo and behold the entry began:

Wool (wul) sb. [Com. Teut. and Indo-Eur. OE wull:. . .]

In a sense I hadn't been wrong at all! So why the thrashing? It was customary to beat pupils for not knowing their tables or their spelling but always there was a list given before or after to help pupils learn the right answer. Today, however, the beating seemed out of proportion to the situation and this failure to help me after the thrashing aroused my suspicions.

Between sobs my memory returned to a conversation with Teacher Danny who taught the newest pupils in "Little A-B-C". She seemed as old as my grandmother and talked constantly, like a mighty waterfall.

A month ago, upon arriving in Wakenaam I had been surrounded and treated with inordinate curiosity by both the pupils and the staff.

"Is where you come from?"

"I born in Mackenzie and grow up in Christianburg," I had replied.

"What Mackenzie like?" was asked by pupils who had never travelled to the opposite end of their island.

"It nice," I mumbled.

4

"Is how long you gun be here?" teachers asked.

"All year."

"Is why?"

"I sittin' scholarship. Dis is me las' try," I explained.

"Is how much brudders and sisters you got?"

"Two. Claire and Keith." Would the questions never end?

"You like living with Mr McGowan and Teacher Dolly?"

"Yes." Which was a lie as I hadn't yet been given a chance to know them but what else could a person say?

"They nice?"

"Umm-humm!" Saying little about much taxed my concentration.

"You clothes nice," they said shyly.

Teacher Danny, a thin, brown woman with long braided white hair, was eager for more intimate details so she threw me this question.

"And is what you gun do," she asked, "if Mr McGowan beat you? He does beat bad, you know."

The granny-looking face seemed to hold enormous sympathy for my possible predicament. Without sifting and weighing my words as before I replied, "I gun go back home to me mother."

Immediately my insides told me that I should never have 'let me mouth open and story jump out'.

Now, weeks later, I couldn't be sure but there was a feeling that this conversation had somehow trickled into the ears of Mr McGowan who had used the pretext of spelling to demonstrate, in the manner of a school play, his power in my life. Matters were now in my hands.

Whimpering softly I slid one hand across my back to touch where it stung. When I looked at my fingers they were covered with warm blood which had come through the stranded organdie blouse. The skin on my back was rising into quite a few welts, my fingertips informed me. I wiped my fingers on the underside of my skirt.

I realised I had no money to return home, a good two days and one night's travelling away. Nor would I, a girl of eleven, have been permitted to leave Wakenaam alone. This beating stated clearly, to the school and to me, Mr McGowan's power and my powerlessness.

For the first time, although I couldn't precisely form the questions I asked myself, "I in a nightmare. Is why?"

My mother's voice seemed to reply in the sweetest tones, "Fo go to Bishops!"

"What is this Bishops!"

"A dream," Mummy's voice seemed to sing.

"I have to take dis beating fo get dis dream?" I asked. "Tell me."

No reply came. I heard my own voice whimpering and smelled, above the Lavender talc, the rank odour of blood.

Two

If you're looking for an eleven year old veteran of settling into another family's household, I was it. It's easy. You take the household tasks, that nobody fights over, without being asked. You empty the white enamel chamber bucket misty morning early into the rickety outhouse, and sweep clean the front and back outside stairs and the unpaved yard. You quickly volunteer to feed the Rhode Island red chickens, wash out their dung covered house and fetch buckets full of cooking water from the well or house vat. Finally, you tidy your room and wash the morning dishes, all before walking out the back yard to school, another fifty metres away. This was my third experience of boarding.

My clothes were always clean and pressed, my shoes polished nightly, hair braided daily and homework done neatly. While I sat at a desk with three other standard four girls, I did completely different work because I was 'sitting scholarship'. Dream, that's all I did, dream of talking. Instead, bookwork had to be written quickly, accurately, quietly and taken to Mr McGowan only. Floggings apart, life on this strange island possessed tremendous joy outside the classroom.

My favourite? Wakenaam food! My first taste of forbidden shark's meat, freshly caught and steamed, was surprisingly pleasant. Such thick white flesh. It was unlike the mass of annoying body bones of Banga Marie or snapper's head. My grandmother, Mudsie, who could conjure a delicious something out of nothing, dutifully stewed the latter in a tomato, celery, onion, pepper and margarine sauce. I felt secretly guilty about breaking one of our sternest religious food taboos by eating fish which had no scales. So, loyally, I drew the line at tempting shrimps and crabs, mud-hopping 'four eyed' fish, crocodiles, turtles and manatees.

Ram goat curry eaten with rice took a lot of getting used to. Pre-historic hassa, which hibernates in mudholes during the dry season and swims into frenzied life with the rains' arrival, was my hands-down favourite although the massala never altogether disguised its mud flavour. Then there was Wakenaam's flavoured bread, kneaded only half as long as Mudsie's, the loaves emerging with a coarser texture.

Old Dee Dee Maarie across from the school's playground baked in a small oval mud oven which sported a domed roof like a mosque's. I learnt to fire the oven's cavity with coconut husks and shells, and scraps of wallaba timber and driftwood, before scraping out the ashes, pushing the twin loaves of dough within and stopping the entrance with a snugly fitted mud-bung. Sister Dolly never knew I baked while visiting Lynette, Dee Dee Maarie's grand-daughter. The bread was a worthy rival, in taste and aroma, of Mudsie's champion aniseed loaf!

On rare occasions, suspecting I'd not be missed, I'd pelt off from our fenced yard to a soursop or custard apple tree I'd sharp-eyed earlier. Sometimes I climbed a foo-foo mango tree, or collected shoes full of jamoons and socks full of West Indian gooseberries. My heart pounded as I condor-eyed all the while for venomous snakes around the rank growth at the tree-roots. Wiser picknee would never have ventured near the trees in their most lunatic dreams.

Imagine an Eden-like, sleepy looking island lolling in the mouth of the eleven kilometre wide Essequibo river. An island of lush vegetation, coconut palms everywhere fanning the blue heavens. Imagine tidy, green rice fields mile upon mile. Unfenced yards with breadfruit, papaya, avocado and carombola trees. Kitchen gardens yielding wrist to elbow length bora beans, purple aubergines, red werri-werri peppers, Kelly-green kalaloo and red tomatoes. The wooden water vats in Fredericksburg, where I lived that fateful year, squandered liquid down moss-covered sides and the trenches were choked with water hyacinth. One could eat off the land by growing staples like cassava, eddoes, yams and dasheens. Fish and wild life were abundant and chickens thrived.

But the McGowan family wished for other foodstuffs and groceries, and I volunteered for the task. I hoped to prove trustworthy and almost adult by shopping wisely for everything on the list. Gradually, weekly Saturday shopping in the adjoining village of Noitgedacht became an ordeal. An East Indian teenager on a bike took to accosting me on the lonely road, making lewd suggestions. Yet, I couldn't bring myself to tell my family about it. Desperate one day, I carried the heavy basket of rice, flour, sugar, oil, butter, soap, plantains, matches, kerosene, milkpowder, hair-vaseline, saltfish, saltbeef, yeast, candles, onions, shoepolish, baking powder and chicken feed, in the midday heat. The five kilometre journey lay before me and I was petrified at the now familiar sight of the slim, shoeless wastrel down the road, sitting motionless on his bike.

A short distance out of the village I ducked into Teacher Vi's yard to tell her of my plight. She was not at home, neither were the men, but an old "auntie" was. Using some cotton material for a belt at her waist, she strapped a sharpened cutlass behind her back, and walked with my basket, speaking in a light-hearted fashion with me. Her round face and thick black plaits, her plump figure and pretty frock, made her look gentle and motherly. Reaching the boy who was still balancing astride his bike pretending to admire a rice field, she let go of the basket and

9

grabbed him, her left hand pulling his pants skywards by his belt, her working woman's right hand holding a fistful of his faded plaid shirt. He and the bike tottered clumsily.

I grabbed his Raleigh men's bike to steady it and awkwardly untied the cutlass from the cloth belt. Auntie let go the shirt and held the gardening implement, the cutlass.

"You see dis what I got in me hand? Eh?" she asked turning the sharp, shiny blade this way and that under his nose as she spoke, while still holding his pants front skywards. He was too stunned to react and I was too goose-fleshed with fear on that otherwise deserted road, to think clearly.

"Ah ent frighten fo use it if I have to! And I know you face. You is from Maria Pleasure's village. Now, if you don't want me to cut off you 'what's its name', don't come near dis gal picknee again. You hear me? Don't even speak to she! Now get on you bike and go 'long you way!" She struck the cross bar, handle and carrier of the bike with resounding clangs, to emphasise her determination. The terrified lad, with downy fuzz on his chin, seen-a-ghost eyes and dirty, broken fingernails, scrambled away. I never saw him again as long as I lived in Wakenaam.

I walked home with fear in my sternum and tried to tell the family what had occurred, but let it go after the first mumble.

That unique school year which began in September 1954 stamped unforgettable growth marks on my mind and body. Certainly I had sprouted a few more inches, but that wasn't all. On a social evening visit to the neighbours I overheard Sister Dolly confiding in Mrs Cannings. Thirty-ish, a born-again Christian and mother of four, Mrs Cannnings always had the family recite Psalm 91 at the end of their meal. Her daughter was slightly younger than me.

"Well, Mona will be a young lady soon," Sister Dolly was saying.

"She's got proper mosquito bites on her chest and fuzz under her arms."

"Fuzz! Under my ARMS! I'm glad that's all she's seen," I whispered to myself. The moment came one morning as I emerged from having a village shower, where you ladle half the bucket of chilly well water over yourself, soap up to fury, then ladle the rest of the cold water over, to rinse off.

"Oh me Lawd!" I said in mild panic. "Sister Dolly?" I called. Then I whispered, "My leg. There on my leg . . ." We did things with safety pins and cotton fabric. I felt neither elation nor fear, no shame either, but a deep gulf of unknowing. How does this happen? Why?

"You mother speak to you?" Uncle Hulbert asked me before I went to school. The question had no meaning because nervous Mummy had, like our Almighty on Mt Sinai, issued many stern orders.

"Don't ever be rude to big people!"

"Don't complain!"

"Remember to say 'Please', 'Thank you' and 'Beg pardon'."

"Don't make yourself a burden to the family, you hear?"

Now, not wishing to be a burden and embarrassed to speak about it to a man, I lied, "Yes Uncle Hulbert."

Precisely what my mother was meant to have said to me I couldn't guess. But I recollected vividly Mudsie, my short, solid, gentle grandmother, speaking passionately but softly to my older sister Claire a year ago in the dim, kerosene lamp lit kitchen.

"Young lady . . . young lady. And don't let no boy interfere with you. Ah don't want you talking 'round no boys. You hear me? You keep away from boys or I'll peel the black off your backside."

That seemed like a joke coming from Mudsie, who never smacked anyone, and who doted so much on Claire she couldn't speak crossly to her. Gentle Claire, my sister who usually burst

11

into tears when cast a harsh look, fled past me distraught and wore a haunted gaze for months afterwards.

Who could shed 'light-without-fear' on me if I turned to them? Lucy, my bench mate with jutting jawbones, and slim Meylene in standard six with brown patches on her teeth? They were older and 'young ladies' already. They wished to be vastly helpful during playtime.

"Is what it called?" We ambled through damp, uncut grass on the play ground.

"My mother does say 'Flowers', but my auntie does say 'Moon rain'," Lucy said.

"I wish I could read about it in a secret book because nobody don't want to tell me about it," Meylene said.

"Is why it does happen?"

"I ent know," each young lady said.

"But is how often it will happen?" I asked. We stopped to pick snodgrass and edible bora-bora berries at the edge of the field.

"Moon after moon," Meylene offered.

"Until when?"

"Until you old," Lucy answered as we spat out the bora-bora skins.

"But like how old?" I wanted to know.

"Like Teacher Danny, me mother say. Den it gun stop by itself," Meylene filled in.

"It don't stop at all, at all?" I was puzzled.

"If it stop is because you getting baby," Meylene explained.

"But you can't get baby unless you do common-ness with your husband," she reassured me.

"Oh!" I said. "What common-ness like?"

"I ent know. You know Meylene?" Lucy asked.

"I hear me mother say it like a plunger. But how it like a plunger, on the side of a Parker pen, when you trying fo get the ink up the pen tube, I ent know," Meylene said. I didn't know either.

"So what gun happen to me now?"

"You gun grow up and look just like you mother," Lucy offered. I didn't want to look like my mother. I wanted to grow into a swan, like Lena Horne, the American jazz singer featured in Mudsie's *Ebony* magazines imported from Chicago.

At hearing the bell's ruffling the morning air we sprinted through the grass to the schoolhouse. The realisation came too late. As my legs pushed my leaping body through the rough clump, blades of razor grass sliced my calves, not badly but enough to draw beads of blood. I wiped the smarting flesh with the hem of my school skirt, lined up with the girls and wished that my mother had spoken to me.

Mysteriously five hard cover books appeared in my bedroom that I shared with Mr McGowan's nephew Frankie. They were *Water Babies, Treasure Island, Westward Ho!, Alice in Wonderland* and *Sex Education* by Cyril Bibby. Frankie read them. I read them too, never truly understood any of them but I liked *Westward Ho!* best.

Three

Trent swept my wide delivery under the school house for four runs.

"Bowl de blasted ball properly! A full pitch, not a wide! You McMahon gal picknee!" he chucked off at me. As Trent Thompson and I studied for Scholarship together we sometimes played together. I scrambled in the dusty crawl space beneath the school building and grabbed the cricket ball.

"Tek dis one den!" I grunted delivering a leg spinner. Trent blasted it beyond the school grounds into Dee Dee Maarie's yard across the road.

"Ah is the great Worrell, Walcott and Weeks put together!" he exulted, naming West Indian cricket heroes and holding up his bat. "Six!" He practised blasting an imaginery delivery into covers while I dashed over to retrieve the battered ball. I could have ambled. There was no traffic. The road sometimes resounded to the odd donkey cart's rattle, but bicycles were a once daily mail service affair and cars a rarity, apart from that of Mr Cannings, our neighbour, the sanitary inspector.

Recrossing the road I saw in the distance a lone man, fair-skinned, with cheese-coloured hair. He had his hands in his pockets and was taking in the view while he sauntered towards us.

"Mr McGowan! Mr McGowan!" I raced in and addressed him formally now that we were in school, "a Backra, — a white man comin' down de road!"

14

"He by Persaud's salt goods shop!" Trent added, bat resting on his shoulder.

Mr McGowan grabbed the iron bell by its polished, wooden handle and rang it insistently, even though we still had ten minutes left of morning tea break. Blast! I'd miss my chance to bat like West Indian Sir Leary Constantine and Trent would miss his chance to bowl like Guianese Sonny Rahmadin. Classes fell into formation at the stairs to the school door, girls and boys in separate lines. Hungry mothers of scrawny children scrambled to beg Teacher Vi to pour into their enamel cups the milk which their children were due to drink as a gift from UNICEF. It was for those suffering from malnutrition. Strict Teacher Vi eagle-eyed the pupils to ensure that they swallowed the cod liver capsule and ate the vitamin filled biscuit. But as the milk was made from milk powder mixed with well water, and was thought to cause diarrhoea, she was lenient about letting parents take their portion home to boil and share among family members. The washed milk pails, the biscuits and cod liver oil were now quickly padlocked into the food cupboard. Pupils sat expectantly at their desks. When the unwary tourist strode casually by, he was stopped and invited off the dusty road into the one-room school building by Mr McGowan.

He was then escorted up to the stage although he wasn't an official, and seated with dignity. The school rose and with Mr Amos, the Deputy Principal, conducting, we sang a nationalist song.

Born in the land of the mighty Rorima,
Land of great rivers and far stretching seas,
So like the mountain, the sea and the river,
Great, wide and deep in all eyes would we be.

Onward, upward, may we ever go,
Day by day in strength and beauty grow,

15

Till at length each of us may show
What Guiana's sons and daughters can be.

Born in the land where men sought El Dorado . . .

Mr McGowan strategically sent a boy up a tree on the school's property to pick two liquid filled coconuts and while the pale visitor waited, he began a speech. I wondered what he could possibly find to tell a total stranger.

"You have come at an historic time to our island of Wakenaam and to our country, British Guiana. We welcome you heartily. This place was settled centuries ago by the Dutch as the place names will inform you—Wakenaam, New Amsterdam, Fredericksburg, Vreed-en-hoop, Den Amstel. The French were here too, at places like La Bonne Intention, Belle Plaine, La Penitence and Versailles. Now, 1954 finds us belonging to Britain with the capital Georgetown and villages like Buxton, Kitty and McKenzie, and I say, this nonsense must stop! This belonging to another nation is a confounded nonsense that must stop!"

The visitor looked bemused and somewhat out-of-place. He shifted in his seat and surveyed us. We scrutinised his curious shoes, strange cheddar-cheese coloured hair, white eyebrows and golden fuzz on his forearm. Mr McGowan filled centre stage like a strong voiced minister in a pulpit.

"Our Guianese people are ready to govern ourselves. We want Self-Government! As you know, we had a general election recently and returned the candidates of our choice, Dr Jagan, Brindley Benn and others. And the British have arrested every last member of our government. Locked up every Man Jack! Without trial! On a remote island called Sibley Hall. And Britain says it has suspended the constitution. Britain says that the people WE want to govern us are communists! Since Britain is telling us who we should not vote for, why did we hold elections at all?

"I say that the constitution was not suspended, it was taken away altogether. That is wrong! Wrong! Unjust!"

16

The school sat holding its breath listening to a heated political speech as fiery as a cane field's burn off. Most of us knew that Mr McGowan could be arrested and jailed that night for voicing those words, especially in a government school, and to a Backra, er . . . a white man. He paced up and down the stage like a lesser Winston Churchill, jabbing the air, sixth finger dancing, and continued.

"I say, the constitution of British Guiana was taken away— the British have treated us with neither justice nor respect. In the past we have responded with slave rebellions. Like the 1823 Rebellion on the Vreed-en-Hoop estate owned by the family of the British Prime Minister Gladstone. We hope for a peaceful change to Self-Government. After all, our people have had enough martyrs like our slave rebellion leader, Quamina Gladstone and his son Jacky . . ." He had even spoken his speech in flawless, 'White people English'.

Mercifully, the boy and the coconuts appeared. Mr McGowan shook the hand of the visitor, we rose and said in unison, "Good Morning Sir!" and the white man whose name and country of origin we did not catch, was led off the stage. He drank his coconut water and ate the soft white flesh in the school yard while Mr McGowan chatted with him. Fear and excitement generated 'ning-ning', a magical heat shimmer, before my eyes. For a while I said to myself, "Lawd! Mr McGowan puttin he head in de jaguar's mouth!"

Not daring to comment openly on his speech, we took out our books, picked up our pencils and prepared for the next lesson. Our insides were quivering.

Fearful events and plentiful food, these spelled Wakenaam to me.

Four

Joan of Arc and Marie Curée were the only towering heroines I had read about, but their lives in far off Europe offered nothing I understood as useful for the everyday battles in my Guianese life. The women of my father's ancestral Black village of Buxton stood on the trainline and stopped the Governor's carriage decades ago. They forced him to accept a petition stating their grievances and were suitably daring, but more formidable than I felt I could be. So too was 'Cutlass Auntie' who'd saved me from that wastrel.

Before departing in December for Christianburg to spend two glorious weeks of Christmas holidays with my family, Mr McGowan had bowled me a 'bumper', his prediction for 1955.

"I can promise yo nothing but blood, sweat, toil and tears!" he'd said, punctuating the line with his smoker's cough. I'd refused to flinch automatically so he'd tried a new ploy. He switched to the race track.

"It's goingta be whip and spur to train yo' into peak condition fo the June exams! Whip and spur! And you gointa haveta make up yo mind fo stay and burn or cut and run! No two ways about that, me gal! This is yo last chance for Scholarship. Yo'll be eleven and a half . . . so, whip and spur it'll be!"

As it was, I'd frantically learnt to spell—through, thorough, bear, beer, bare, whether, weather. Then I'd used them inappropriately and received a caning. I'd memorised up to twenty-five times tables without being told to but still was whacked for not remembering how to calculate the hypotenuse of a triangle. Moreover, story writing held unexpected hazards. Imitating the style of *Westward Ho!* which I'd just read, I tried some fancy writing. Mr McGowan took one look at the opening line and bellowed, "This is not your writing!"

"No Uncle Hulbert," I murmured. "I wrote it myself." The whole school froze watching; he was pushing back his chair, his hand was stretching for the cane.

"Don't lie! Yo did copy this!" he insisted.

What could I say? He demanded excellent writing from me or I'd be caned, but would shame and cane me before the school if the writing seemed too stylish to be mine.

"Yes, Uncle Hulbert," I lied. "I copied it." If I'd escaped a caning that time many more beatings awaited me. I knew I had to convince Mummy not to return me to Wakenaam in the New Year.

Journeying from Wakenaam to Leguan to Parika to Vreed-en-hoop to Georgetown, I seemed insulated in a pod of three dozen mosquito nets layered each atop the other, so unaware was I of the launches, train, bus and steamer speeding me along. "Is how I gun ask Mummy?" my mind wrestled with the question.

The first time, at seven, when I'd been sent away with Claire to Georgetown to board with Aunt Carrie and Uncle Jim in their huge home, which later became a high school, I'd hated it. Although as a teenager Mummy had herself boarded there and had retained fond memories of the family, now Claire and I alone were put to help in the kitchen. We were seated at a humble oil-skin covered, rickety, painted side table. All the others sat at a highly polished, twelve seat, mahogany table. And we were teased and bullied at the capital's most exclusive prep school, Owen's Private School, where most of the other pupils were white. Nor could we inform Mummy of our distress. All our letters were read by Aunt Carrie, 'for spelling errors' before being mailed home. She needed boarders to make ends meet.

Secretly we'd whispered our troubles into the ear of the washer woman who collected our grubby kitchen dresses and returned them washed, starched, ironed and folded. A former servant of my grandmother's, she loyally wrote home explaining that the state of our clothes betrayed our treatment as kitchen hands rather than as boarders. One gloriously sunny morning, like a rehearsal for the arrival of the Messiah, Mummy came to pack and shift us to the haven of our great aunt's, to the home of Lydia Maud Jones. Although jubilant, we questioned her as we walked, suitcases on the bicycle carriers.

"Why can't we come home with you to Christianburg?" We spoke Properly then.

"You got fo get a good education, love, and Georgetown schools really good. See how nice you just talk to me? Like English people? Dat's what ah paying all dis money for, so you could talk nice and represent yourself and have people respect you. You got fo board here and study," Mummy explained. "And get a good education," she repeated.

Recalling that time four years previously, I planned to use my clothes as articles of persuasion. Mummy met me at the Georgetown wharf as I stepped off the steamer from Vreed-en-Hoop. We kissed and admired each other then hurried through the bustling Stabroek market adjoining the wharf.

"Your great-great grandmother, Sarah Coderington, had a fish stall in this market, 1900s about," Mummy commented, waving and pointing at crab and fish sellers, fruit vendors and basket makers. "She made money though. When Sarah died they buried her from her own home . . . in Worthmanville."

The following day we steamered to Christianburg. In the gossiping, cooking, shopping, baking, house cleaning, visiting and partying before Christmas, I showed Mummy, who was herself a schoolteacher, the organdie blouses. The fabric on the backs was frayed by lashes and discoloured by blood.

"Mummy, Mr McGowan beat me till the blouse shred-up," I began, displaying the blouses over my legs.

"I gun sew you better blouses outta strong cotton. Dese ones too light," she replied. "But he teaching you good for Scholarship. Nuh chile?"

"He does teach me good but . . ."

"I have no doubt that you gun win Scholarship with McGowan. He son win Scholarship and Mrs Trotz daughter, Dorothy, win wid he too. So, don't mind he a bit strict I know he is a good, good teacher."

"But Mummy, tek a look at me back," I said, untying my sash and unbuttoning the dress back to show her a mass of old scars and fresh welts. "I can't sleep on me back. Only on me front. It does bleed all the time," I said.

But Mummy was blinder to my back than a bat in the noon sun and deafer to my pleas than a tree trunk; so seductive was the whispered, golden promise of Scholarship.

"He got fo beat you fo make you learn," she said in tones as sweet as a yellow-tail bird's call. "He taking a interest in training you fo pass Scholarship. Understand?"

Mummy's ideas seemed attuned to that inscription I'd read in one of her old Royal Readers, saved from primary school.

If you cannot work without the rod
Then you are a slave!

For whom was I working though?

My voice grew Macaw-hoarse from crying. Mummy avoided me for days if she suspected that I'd pursue the subject. Desperation, however, drove me to voice my shilling's worth again. I felt belted to the boundary for a mighty six by her response.

"You is the best thing complaining, eh? After all, Life ent easy!" Mummy snapped.

Gentle Claire, my sister of the soft eyes and smooth ebony face, now thirteen and at the local Eccles High School across the river, shared my misery.

"Girl, Mona, don't cry. Mummy do the same thing to me. One day she marched over to the high school to Miss Blair, me French teacher, and say 'Miss Blair, is alright with me if you was to cane Claire. I is not one o' these mothers who would meet you on the road, scramble you, collar you off, cuff you up, rip off you dress, knock you with your own shoe heel and half-hang you if you was to beat Claire. You is to tear she tail if she don't do she work properly! I don't mind at all. I want Claire to learn she lessons!'."

Miss Blair, one of those rare persons who had gone to University, hated and avoided canings, which was lucky for Claire. My doom, on the other hand, was sealed.

Running errands for my great grandmother and taking long soothing swims in the Demerara river stopped me from thinking. The holiday calypsoes were drowned out by the remembered whirr of the cane. Despite my love of food I ate distractedly. Rum drenched, black and fruity Christmas cake tasted like rubber. Fragrant coconut ice-cream sat on my tongue like soap, and spicy cinnamon-and-cow's-heel-pepperpot was no more inviting than a banana peel.

I was as enthusiastic to return to Wakenaam as I would have been to visit a burial ground, when the dark-time jumbies danced on a covered-moon night. What would the 'star-girls' of my favourite films have done if they'd dreaded a place?

What would Esther Williams, Virginia Mayo, Janet Leigh or Barbara Stanwick have said? Silent tears ruled the final day before my return.

"I don't want to go back. Oh Gaaawd, I don't want to . . ."

I pleaded with Mummy before dinner. After dinner she said, "I gun buy you a bike if you win Scholarship."

My watchful great grandmother Adrianna said nothing but made me sleep in her cramped iron bed with her that night.

Well, "God don't come, but He does send", as the saying goes.

Send Nora, he did. In the New Year an orphaned, ten and a half year old poor relation came to be educated and brought up by Sister Dolly. Short haired, square jawed, she was always nervous, tended to stammer and she was a bed-wetter. She shared the bedroom with Frankie and me and was the focus of the McGowan's attention. The beatings were shared between us, which was some sort of a silver lining. And I had a girl to be friends with.

"Dolly! Dolly! Oh Gaawd! Help me!" Uncle Hulbert's voice trumpeted. It was shortly after midnight. We awoke but stayed in our bedrooms as the feet thunder-clapped up the front stairs.

"Oh migawd, you bleeding bad! Wha' happened Hulbert?" Sister Dolly's voice sounded frightened.

"Some men waylaid me while I was coming home. They tried fo chop me up with their cutlass . . ." he coughed and sat down heavily.

"But where was you?" Sister Dolly probed. "Come. Tek off this shirt."

"At Teacher Vi's house."

"At this late hour? What you was doing there?" she dug further.

"Well, as I was leaving fo go away to Georgetown tomorrow. I wanted fo tell she how fo run the school while I away," he said, panting.

"Steady. Let me get your arm out, but Mr Amos is you Deputy, not Vi. He . . . ." she countered.

"I don't want Amos in charge of me school."

23

"But you self too, Hulbert!" Sister Dolly spoke heatedly. "You couldda talked to Vi after school, you couldda talked to she in the school self, or at home here. You couldda give me a message fo Vi. You didn't have no business fo go round to she house at this hour o' the night." There was a pause filled with water being poured into an enamel basin, soap, dettol, gauze, cotton-wool, ointment, scissors, bandages, sympathy, anger and shuffling footsteps, all tending his wounds.

"Look, is only Dettol. It won't sting." Pause. "What so private anyway that you got fo go to she house at midnight to talk about it?" The orator made no reply. "And who attacked you?" Sister Dolly's voice sounded anxious.

"The husband Teacher Vi used to be married to, an East Indian, and one of he men friends. They were hiding in the bushes by the road, but luckily it was dark, and they missed a lot of blows."

"Don't tell me one thing more, Hulbert! Stay quiet! I don't know why you talking school business at midnight . . . Oh Goooood!" She groaned. I heard a pained rather than a frosty distant woman. "You see how people can misunderstand what you do! See how they jumped to conclusions! You couldda been killed! This is aaaawful!"

Nora and I felt sorry but had no idea how to behave politely in the morning. We wished to appear neither forward nor uncaring; perhaps it would be best to 'see nothing, hear nothing, say nothing'.

We wore straight faces next morning, said our "Good mornin's" and resolutely noticed nothing out of the ordinary. That week Nora learnt that she was returning to Den Amstel.

"But is what I do Sister Dolly?" she asked, puzzled.

"Is what you ent do!" she was informed. "You didn't have the eyes to notice Uncle Hulbert. You didn't have the heart to feel for him! You didn't have the mouth to ask he how he was!" I wished to set the record straight but bit my tongue. Handing

Nora one of my exercise books as a going away present I watched her silent tears of pained confusion. Secretly I fully expected a time of torment later. How I'd miss Nora. To my relief however, from that fateful night onward Uncle Hulbert lost his desire to cane me ever again.

I took my turn as a senior girl pupil to sweep the school house with a coconut broom, one afternoon before dusk. "What happened to Mr McGowan?" Teacher Danny who was on late duty, asked. She appeared absorbed in threading a tapestry needle with the Amerindian raffia we called 'tibi-siri'. Neat piles of hand work lay on a long desk in front of her. There was a wealth of woven pink and white table mats, delicate purses, window shades of coconut fronds, slippers and church hats which she had taught the pupils to fashion during handicraft lessons. These would be sold at the coming annual gala to raise funds for school projects.

"I could ask him for you, Teacher Danny, and tell him that you would like to find out. You want me to do that for you?" I swept the dust through the front door.

"No. No. No," Teacher Danny whispered quickly, "but you mean to say you don't know?" She barely raised her eyes from the hanks of coloured tibisiri.

"Don't know what, please, Teacher Danny?" I asked, continuing to sweep down the front steps.

"What happened to McG. You ent see the bandages on he forehead? He shoulder? He neck? Some with blood?" she pointed out, needle and tibisiri poised.

"What bandages, Teacher Danny? Where?" I asked, poker faced, stopping to look at her before picking up the dusting cloth.

"Oh!" her voice trailed off and she concentrated on stitching on the braided strands trimming the slippers she was finishing. I continued to dust the teachers' desks and to lock up the windows.

With Nora's departure I was sharply aware of another New Year's ritual: Sister Dolly taking the morning roll of the Standard Ones.

"Maureen Paul."

"Here Miss."

"Betty Persaud."

Silence.

"Betty Persaud."

Stubborn silence.

"Betty Persaud."

Cold, furious silence. "Whack! Whack!" the cane would fall.

"Answer me when I call your name!"

"Waaaaaaaaaa!" Kunia Persaud, of East Indian heritage, would wail daily, her voice ribboning through the one room building. The school day had not really begun, there was even afternoon roll call to come.

Finally, Hindu Mrs Persaud left her salt goods shop down the road and came, round bellied pregnant. She wore a clean pressed but ill-fitting floral dress and had clean, oiled, bare feet. Her head was tied in a lily-white embroidered cotton cloth. She brought Kunia by the hand and stood, country confident, before the well-dressed authority of Teacher Dolly. No parent had ever come on this matter before while I was at the school.

The school waited to observe the test match. Sister Dolly nodded a greeting with a superior air.

One on the off side, fine delivery.

"Marnin', Teacher McGowan."

Mrs Persaud replied to the bowling. Touched with the bat and it has dribbled away. Persaud. No runs.

Sister Dolly drew herself up wordlessly and faced Mrs Persaud.

26

Full pitch, with a slight turn at the last moment.

"Teacher McGowan, ah come fo say to you, na beat dis picknee. She real, true-to-God name ah Kunia Persaud." Mrs Persaud's voice rang clearly in very broken English.

Persaud, . . . forward defensively. And the crowd is enjoying this test on a fine pitch at Bourda . . .

Running in from the Pavilion end, good speed, McGowan . . . swift delivery . . . sends down a googly . . .

"But dis is a Christian school. Fredericksburg Church of Scotland School!" Sister Dolly announced. "And if your child wants to come to dis particular school she will have to have a Christian name. She can even have a great-up name like Princess, or Elizabeth or Victoria or Margaret."

Ah! The names of royalty, I thought. Everyone was accustomed to East Indian pupils with names like Jagdeo or Surujwattie in the playground, being called John and Sarah in the classroom.

But . . . Persaud swings . . . turns it powerfully. Lofted it . . . cracked that ball clear out of the pavilion! Played with tremendous confidence for six!

"Well then Teacher McGowan, call she 'Daughter Persaud' and she will answer you. 'Daughter' is a good name in de English language, and she is me diamond of a daughter." The voice was strong, conceding nothing.

"Daughter Persaud?" Mrs Persaud cooed.

"Here Miss," chimed six year old Kunia in a perfectly executed, obviously rehearsed demonstration.

"See?" Mrs Persaud exulted. "See!".

The crowd, that outwardly silent school of one hundred and fifty pupils, gives a deafening heartfelt cheer.

"Don't lick she no-more Teacher McGowan. And if she do anything wrong, Teacher McGowan, just send a message to the shop and I will tend to she."

Persaud has given a tremendous performance at the crease . . . has declared, and walks back to the Pavilion bat in hand. A very respectable score that, in front of this appreciative crowd at Bourda Cricket Ground.

Then she waddled out of the school, her ill fitting dress swishing. The school sat in silence, not daring to smile. Cheering within. And stunned.

This test match has surely set a record here . . .

Kunia-Daughter-Persaud was never again caned.
She wasn't Joan of Arc, Marie Curée or Cutlass Auntie, but Mrs Persaud that day towered heroically in my eleven-year-old Guianese eyes.

Five

Zeg! Zeg! Zeg!
Mama zeg if you're zegging

I sang that and other calypsoes constantly and danced discreetly travelling across the eleven kilometre wide Essequibo river and on the long train ride from Parika to Suddie, up North. Most of us in the county of Essequibo assembled that June in Suddie, to sit the scholarship exam at Suddie Primary School. High spirits, slight apprehension and determination accompanied me from Wakenaam.

Our chaperon, Mrs Thompson, Trent's mother, brought the youngest pair of her five children, shy girls of four and two. Trent struggled with the family suitcase which contained the clothes for four people for four days. I lugged mine, our cassava bread, fruit, ginger beer in a bottle, plastic cups and fried snapper in an expertly woven picnic basket. Mrs Thompson fussed over the girls and the presents for the friend at whose place we would lodge. She fed us regularly after saying fervent grace before meals, and settled us in smoothly into her friend's home at nightfall. The friend was a single mother of two appealing young children.

The least prosperous of the three counties in British Guiana, Essequibo's villages and school wore the badges of survival but no medals of prosperity. There were unsealed roads, small unpainted wooden houses, hardly abundant kitchen gardens, far from plump domestic animals and thin looking people. The once-painted school needed repairs to walls and windows but was tidy inside and felt friendly.

Saturday morning of the exam Trent and I, in pressed uniforms with our exam numbers in hand, made the short walk to the exam centre next door.

"You nervous Trent?" I asked. We were the only pupils from our school.

"Yeah. Bad. You?" He sucked in his breath, changed his ruler, fountain pen, blotting paper, pencil and eraser to his left hand and smoothed his sweaty right palm over his khaki shorts. Trent had an outgoing personality. He was solidly built with bunched teeth and tightly curled reddish hair. Trent studied hard but seemed only to come alive and display his natural talent on the cricket pitch.

"I O.K.," I said, adding, "I wish you all you wish yourself!" which was an auntie's favourite wish. With roughly eighty other eleven-year-old pupils we took our seats silently. The 1955 National Scholarship Examination began.

Deep breaths. Concentrate. Use your times tables. Check twice before you write. Count on your fingers if you have to. Try to be accurate, speed is not all! Write deliberately. The Mental Arithmetic taxed me although I was ready for it.

On to the Written Arithmetic, which was not my strongest subject. Leave time at the end for rechecking. Use your tables for the long divisions. Remember to round up the number in doing the percentages if they ask you for 12 1/2. Ah, I remember this one, you use pi-R-squared-H to work it out. Check that you've numbered the sums correctly. You've done this so many times before, make sure you recheck twice. Measure accurately with your ruler. Try hard. You don't have another chance.

After the morning tea break we were back for the English

test, a combination of a comprehension test, language exercises and an essay. The composition was a challenge as the topics seemed outside my experience but I chose to write on 'A day in my life as a fishmonger'. I embroidered from my observations of fishsellers in Wakenaam and from what I had heard of the life of my great-great grandmother, Sarah Coderington from Barbados. It was to be the only time all day that I was pleased with what I had written. Too nervous doing the dictation to know how I had fared, "I simply couldn't spell!" I told Trent later.

Lunchtime was followed by the intelligence test. Experts said that a person could never study to prepare for it. You had to 'live widely, read newspapers, devour books, listen to the radio and talk with one's parents daily' to answer those questions about everyday life. I mainly studied old intelligence test papers. I missed a few on that test but my spirits were still buoyant at the three o'clock bell. Trent had a hollow look in his large hazel eyes and was withdrawn and silent. Mrs Thompson was quiet too. We put the exam papers into our suitcases to go over with Mr McGowan.

On Sunday Mrs Thompson shepherded us to the local wooden Protestant church and prayed passionately for our success. There was little to do in Suddie, nothing to see after dark in a village without electricity or street lights, so we gave our house presents, said our thanks and prepared for an early start for Wakenaam on Monday morning. In the dark bedroom, looking through the window at the black velvet sky, carelessly fire-hosed with diamonds, the memory of my Christianburg home and family crowded my mind, perhaps because I could now afford to permit myself these thoughts.

"You sweep upstairs yet? No?" I was hearing the voice of my seventy-year-old great-grandmother Adrianna, thundering. "Just now I gun sweep it, Granny Adrianna," I whimper in my best five-and-a-half year old voice. Back would boom the

31

orders. "Not a bit o' 'Just now'! Do it right now! Get the long pointer broom to sweep the stairs, and don't miss sweeping out the corners. And dust down the furniture!"

Old battleaxe. Granny Adrianna was my mother's-mother's-mother. She was the only child brought over from Barbados by Sarah Coderington, in the 1880s, to have survived into adulthood.

"When you finished, fetch a bucket of rain water from the tanks fo wash up all the breakfast glasses and de pots and all the other wares! Then come and help me at the river. Ah got Brother Stuart's clothes fo wash, starch, iron and deliver by tonight if ah want me three dollars fo spend this week."

Granny Adrianna had eyes of ink and hair of smoke. She was frail-looking but steely. I resembled her in temperament and looks and we worked as an agreeable team. While I swished the pants in the river to rinse out the soap Granny Adrianna entertained me with centuries-old rehearsed 'soaps'. Jonah, right here before my eyes, thrown from one of our launches, was being swallowed by a whale. Pharaoh's armies were drowned, chariots and soldiers all, right over there in the channel of our dangerous Demerara River.

We'd lather and beat the sheets and shirts on the sand. Then Moses, Saul and David would win battle after fierce battle while we rinsed and blued the white items. Royalty, King Solomon, Queen Esther and Jonathan, dealt shrewdly with their opponents as we starched and hung the clothes on the paling fence in our yard behind Mudsie's commercial bakery. The blistering equatorial sun would have the clothes dried and a little faded in about four hours. It remained only for us to press the week's laundry with sizzling irons heated on the glowing charcoal in the coalpot, while Joshua's men toppled the walls of Jericho with blasts on their rams' horns. The air reeked of sweat, hair oil, starch and of candle-wax, which we ran over the bottoms of the irons to make them float smoothly over the laundry. I could smell a suggestion of woodsmoke from the charcoal.

32

Before we both set off with the neatly folded clothes in a clean white flour-bag tablecloth, we'd bathe with Pear's soap, and dress in clean, well pressed street clothes. Our jet black chests sported the faintest white dust of Yardley's Lavender talc, our hair lay smoothly brushed. Our appearance was, after all, the best advertisement for our business!

Joseph, finding his way into Egypt as a newly bought slave, would travel with us as far as Stuart's path. There Granny Adrianna collected her three dollars from Sister Stuart. The missionary's wife from Scotland, her face the colour of edible cheese, always spoke a few friendly, pass-de-time words in a language that drifted like the racket of corrugated iron flapping on the roof in a gusty wind. Neither of us knew how to reply to words we didn't understand, but we smiled to show we took her words as friendly. We 'sanga-banga-ed' home swaying down the unlit country road and singing into the black, friendly night, 'Jerusalem the Golden with milk and honey blessed . . .'

This sky in Suddie reminded me so much of Granny Adrianna.

In the morning I journeyed, tired and completely lost in my reverie, in a silence so uncharacteristic that it unnerved the Thompsons. I had done what Mummy had prepared me for and for which I had been sent away to train since the age of seven.

Six

"How you do in de exams?" Sister Dolly enquired.

"I passed!" I announced, bursting with confidence.

"You nothing like Dorothy, with yo boasting!" Sister Dolly flung back scornfully. Dorothy had lived with the family the previous year, had sat scholarship and passed and her sainted memory was now the new force of correction.

"When Dorothy came back last year she said, 'I tried'. Not, 'I passed!'" Sister Dolly scolded.

I thought, "So why expect Dorothy's reply from Mona?" but I stared at the wooden floor and said as much as a mahogany tree does while it's growing.

Without being told so, it was clear that I was expected to remain until the end of the school year in Wakenaam, rather than return to Christianburg immediately. My mind became increasingly preoccupied with yearning for my best friends, Granny Adrianna and the Demerara River.

Visiting school friends was forbidden from my first days in Little A-B-C as a five year old. I was expected to come straight home from Christianburg school, the way Claire always had.

"Girl picknee mustn't learn fo stray bout de place!" Mudsie cautioned, "Bad things could happen!"

Mummy, also, was furious that I had roamed after school to see a sluice gate nearby, damming up a creek, or that I'd hunted turtle's eggs and giant toads, or had gone to feed Mrs Allicock's

34

pet tapir or to say "Pretty Polly" to Mrs D'Anjou's macaw and toucans. The world was so fascinating!

"I regret I licked yo feet in de dew-grass every mornin' when you was slow fo walk," Mummy confessed about her superstitious efforts. "Now yo walking far and wide like that wandering Syrian." She was referring to the Lebanese pedlar who came around twice a year to the households. He displayed a heart-skipping oriental bazaar of silks, linens, laces, ribbons, velvets, rich cottons, brooches and brass-ware which he humped around in his back-bundle like a giant turtle's house. It was a strange way to carry things; Granny Adrianna and the fish sellers and market women always transported heavy bundles on their heads.

So, my best friend through my childhood grew to be the unfailingly bath-warm, mineral-dyed-brown, dangerous Demerara River. It was a stone's throw from Mudsie's cake shop and bakery across the road, and gave its name to coarse brown sugar crystals, Demerara sugar. Mudsie and Granny Adrianna could see where I was. For me, as long as I stayed where my feet could touch the sand, it was a safe, warm world. I could float upon its huge steamer swells, dive-bomb it from a cocoa tree, somersault and backstroke through it, collect floating flowers, and holler and sit upon driftwood, for hours. No, for years!

Occasionally I'd dare to go out further, into the channel, on a corkwood tree trunk of driftwood, or I'd steal a beached Amerindian dugout canoe which someone from outside the village had left while she went shopping. But the channel was a fearsome place. In it were rips, motor launches, steamers and paddle ferry canoes. Rafts of timber bound for the sawmills often passed through it, and Canadian tankers barged down to the capital laden with bauxite ore gouged from our mines. You needed a stout heart to love the river, for if that were not enough, other dangers were water camoudi snakes, catfish with vicious spiny feelers, stingrays, electric eels, piranha which bite through your bones and . . . de Massa Kura Man! All the grownups warned me never to go near his water-lair in the channel because, "De Massa Kura Man does pull people under de waves and keep dem dere as he servants, working forever!" That's why I kept near the sand beach.

When again would I swim in the safe shallows of the Demerara?

The headmaster's house at Wakenaam sat well off the ground on stilts, traditional style, with long stairs up to the front and back doors. One misty morning as I swept the dusty yard around and beneath the house with a coconut broom I heard on Radio Demerara the voice of Ayube Hamid announcing the results of the scholarship exams to the nation. The country waited eagerly to hear which of its children had passed the eleven plus exam, an ordeal most children between ten and twelve years were trained to undergo.

"Scholarship winners for Demerara, girls . . . Allison Kwang . . .99.6 percent," Demerara, the county with the capital, Government House, the largest shopping centres and the important bauxite industry. It had the most political and economic clout, the largest population, apparently the finest schools, and the highest pass marks required for scholarship, 90-100 percent. Or so the gossip decreed.

The roll call for girls and boys ended. Then Ayube, a very ebullient personality, announced Berbice County's boy and girl winners whom, we understood, needed between them 85 and 100 percent to pass. Berbice county was second in wealth and influence. By this time I had crept up the front stairs to the landing attached to the front door to hear the radio clearly.

In Essequibo, the poorest county, we understood that you needed only 80 percent and above to win a pass. Then Ayube announced, "The winners in Essequibo county are . . . Mona Williams 93.7 percent . . ."

I screamed, "Oh Gaaawd! Ah win! Ah win! Ah win!" I flew down the long stairs in two leaps, skirt flying up to expose my white cotton undies. I was screaming, dancing, brandishing the coconut broom, raising dust in a wild zegging dance. My mind's eye saw me as performing an ancient, tribal, African-ritual victory dance. Then my bony black legs raced up the back stairs, I heard my voice scream to Mr McGowan, "Oh Gaaawd, ah win! Ah win Uncle Hulbert! Ah win!"

He strode towards me, English imported dressing-gown carelessly thrown on, clutching his pyjamas in one hand and bellowing, "Congrats girl! congrats!" He pumped my hand furiously.

Sister Dolly continued to listen, stock still, silently, until the last name was announced, impervious to the mayhem.

"Well, yo win," she said flatly.

Frankie came out of our bedroom, stared at me in disbelief with a faint half smile but said nothing. All the same I knew in that moment what pure, kiss-the-sky joy was, and I knew I would never forget the imprint of that feeling on my dancing body as long as I drew breath.

"Did Mummy, like everybody else in British Guiana, hear the announcement on her Pye radio?" I wondered. "Would she listen to the rebroadcast of the names at the midday and 7 pm news on Radio Demerara? Would the people at her school congratulate her? Would Mudsie and Granny Adrianna be proud of me? Would my father's family hear of my success?" Right now, however, I had to get through this triumphant day at my own school:

"Trent, I sorry bad that you didn't get through," I consoled my cricket mate. "I know you tried you best." Trent nodded silently.

Although I was bubbling with joy like over-ripe ginger beer, there was a duty to avoid inviting criticism.

37

"You glad you win Scholarship, chile?" Meylene beamed.

"Heh! Heh!" I giggled. Uncle Hulbert glanced my way and listened.

"You gun be a Bishops gal now, you know," Teacher Danny enthused by way of congratulations. "You glad?"

"Heh! Heh! Heh!" I responded, looking around and catching Sister Dolly sharp-eyeing me. Safety lay in studying hard at Maths and English until the term ended. I cried at night with longing to be home. I ached with the disappointment of a triumph celebrated with no-one.

"We gun have a fire-ass party! You gun get one send off!" friends and teachers promised at the end of the school year in July. Teacher Vi, brown hued and stylish, hefted in a bucketful of bittersweet mauby brew. Other teachers brought covered baskets of coconut buns, pineapple tarts, cheese straws and mince patties. Teacher Danny had made piles of coconut ice, cooked in Demerara sugar. Someone lent us a stack of the latest 78 calypso records and a battery operated record player. Mr McGowan hung the hissing gas tilley lamp from the rafters of the school which had no electricity. The glow was soft and romantic.

Could these be the familiar unpainted school house walls, now festooned with crêpe paper chains of a dozen colours? How friendly the space seemed, cleared of desks and benches and blossom-covered in balloons, sprays of Queen of flowers, jam jars of perfumy frangipani blooms and bright hued hibiscus flowers. Everyone wore Sunday best and shoes for the party. I simply wore my plaid hair ribbons and black patent leather shoes. The revellers were mostly pupils of African descent. Lucy and I outlaughed, outdanced and even outcried one another in turns; zegging, whirling, stomping, winding and singing with the calypso record at top volume.

Come Puunksy come go home,
Come Puunksy come alone,
Come Darlin', stay at home
Leh me play on your gramophone!

Then we let out naughty belly laughs.

We zegged farewell to Fredericksburg school. Plump, dark, loyal Lucy, because she had completed two years' work in one year, finishing standard five at fourteen and had got a job as a servant. Meylene was leaving standard six at fourteen and I was sailing away in the morning.

Particularly sweet memories of Wakenaam are of my leaving it. Dee Dee Maarie and Lynette gave me a bag full of sweet orange-yellow mangoes for the journey. Suitcase packed with a few clothes and my exercise books, I said a formal farewell to the McGowans at the launch wharf, thanking them for helping me to win the scholarship. I would now be able to attend High School which in 1955 was neither free nor compulsory. I was lucky to get one of about sixty free places for girls in the nation. I promised to write. However, gratitude for my success was always overpowered by the smell of blood and the memory of pain whenever I tried to put pen to paper. Thus that letter of thanks was never sent.

Four hours of land and river travel, past villages with Dutch names like Nora's 'Den Amstel', past sugarcane plantations, coconut groves and rice fields under cultivation, and I arrived at Georgetown's main wharf to a smartly dressed, loud voiced, joy-crazy Mummy.

"How you do nuh chile?" Mummy asked, kissing me.

"Ah all right," was all I could manage. I longed to say more at an appropriate time but wondered if Mummy would ever listen.

"Oh Lawd! I couldn't walk down the street at home in peace, all dis last month!" Mummy pretended to complain.

"All the neighbours stoppin me fo say, Eh, Eh! Mrs Williams! Ah hear you girl chile name pon de Radio! She win Scholarship! Congrats! And you do all o dat by youself without them picknee father helping you fo bring dem up! Look how God is good nuh Mrs Williams? You picknee make you proud! Congrats! She gun go to de white people school now she get Scholarship!". The strange thing was that Mummy's eyes seemed haunted with fear while her voice spilled joy.

Much later I learnt the reason, Mrs Grant, the community big-wig's wife.

"She mad like if she push hot pepper up she . . .! She gone and write to the Education Department, to the Authorities fo complain. She want them fo take away you Scholarship. Cancel it!"

"Why?" I trembled.

"She saying that it's not fair. She saying that Demerara children going all the way to Essequibo fo sit the Exam is trickery. Dorothy did it. And now you did it. She think that they goin' to Essequibo fo qualify with the lower pass mark, with 80 percent instead of 90 percent." Mummy looked totally distressed.

"But Mummy, I win wid a Demerara pass mark. I got 93 percent. I even topped Essequibo county with the best marks for both the boys and the girls. I couldda win with that mark here, in Demerara!"

"Well God don't wear pyjamas . . . he neither slumbers nor sleeps. He's in the midst o this. We gun see me chile. We gun see." Mummy said bravely. For weeks as I waited to enter Bishops Mummy woke me up early for prayer together.

"Deliver me, O Lord, from the evil man . . ."
"Keep me, O Lord from the hands of the wicked." Psalm 140.

Or,

"Lord, thou hast been our dwelling place in all generations"
her favourite, Psalm 90.

Seven

"What Bishops like Mudsie?" I asked, hoping there were neither canes nor floggings.

"It de best school in BG. All de big shot people's children go there. Like de people round de Governor. De big business people, de sugar estate managers and de rich white people, their children. Only a few of our people's children they let in, like your cousin Vadney Neblett, and de Shackleford girls and high-up Anglican Church people." I was not persuaded.

"Look, when you come outta dat school you can get a good job anywhere just by saying, 'Ah went to Bishops'. You won't be worried-all-de-time poor; 'a distressed backside on a broken po' poor." Mudsie always explained things so clearly! I felt utterly intimate with Mudsie, I wanted to confide the inconceivable.

"I don't want to go to Bishops! I hope I never go away to school. I want to be near Granny Adrianna and the river." I hemmed and hawed, but I couldn't find the Mrs Persaud kind of nerve to speak my mind, so I finally asked, "What they does do inside the school?"

No one knew for certain what occurred in that exclusive school-heaven but, observing that it was 9 a.m., Granny Adrianna went down to the river with the week's laundry of another church family. Mudsie bustled away to the bakery to knead the troughful of white dough for the third time, before 'panning it off' into loaf tins of various sizes. Mudsie was true to her

41

motto, "Breadbaking must continue even if Good Friday falls on a Tuesday."

Mummy remained to continue the Bishops dialogue and ventured, "I think they will teach you Latin, amo-amas-amat," showing off what she remembered from twenty years before.

Like an earth tremor gleefully rattling the crystal on Mudsie's chiffonier, our house was a-tremble with laughter and activity, preparation and joy. Mummy sewed the Bishops uniform of one four-gored, green cotton skirt, although the school regulations required two skirts, and three short-sleeved white blouses. We scraped together the money for the regulation brown leather shoes and white ankle socks, tennis shoes and green woollen (woollen!) knickers. Mudsie came to the rescue with the panama hat and monogrammed hatband, school tie and bullock hide bookbag. Granny Adrianna secretively placed on my lap a bulging knotted hankie full of hoarded copper cents and pennies, enough to buy a new bra. Dressed for the family to admire I looked like a boarding school character straight out of an English schoolgirls' magazine, except 'in black face'.

A government prize of a book allowance provided the second hand texts and exercise books, the government scholarship paid my school fees but the till was empty before Mummy could rise to the prestigious green woollen school blazer which sported the school's crest, a tennis racquet and hockey stick. And the promised bicycle? Well. Suitable for a six year old, it wheeled me easily enough from 'doorpost to gatepost' but earned me constant teasing from total strangers.

"Lokka big gal pun a lil bike," they jeered. "Monkey pun Iron! Baboon pun Steel! Ha!Ha!Ha!Ha!

Speak of my black mother being bled white! The three children, someone had decided, should all be educated together in Georgetown. Claire had to be kitted out too, to attend Central High School, founded and run by a Chinese family. They were the Lucks, — 'who have de musical prodigy son'. My brother Keith, a disarming ten year old, the runaway favourite and solitary young male in our usually female household, was to attend a church administered primary school, Cormenius Moravian. He had only one pair of khaki school pants, that slide-on-his-bottom, rough-housing prankster! Keith was training to sit scholarship in his eleven-plus year.

Bishops filled me with awe and excitement from the very first day. The wooden, three levelled, roughly Z shaped school for about 500 girls exuded an air of English colonial gentility. There was something overwhelming about the framed Turners, Constables, Gainsboroughs and Michaelangelo reproductions in the main foyer. The highly polished wooden staircase curved up to the first floor where dust free mahogany furniture was everywhere, as were the unobtrusive aproned black servants bringing morning and afternoon tea to the staffroom. The quiet speech, 'a sign of refinement, girls', barely above a whisper even when classes were being taught, was unnerving. But who would not feel privileged in a world of freshly painted cream coloured classroom walls, highly polished wooden floors swept daily by servants and tasteful floral arrangements in the public reception areas. The classrooms were spacious and well lit and each pupil had an individual desk and chair.

The school, bejewelled with glass windows, lounged on sprawling hectares of well kept grounds behind neatly painted white picket fences. Basdeo, the East Indian groundsman, maintained perfectly manicured tennis courts, netball quads and a sportsfield. He was everywhere, and always rolling the rain-sodden courts or sprinkling the parched ground, cutting, weeding, transplanting and trimming hedges. He delivered bouquets of white lilies to the staff room, long stemmed roses to the Head mistress's office and anthuriums to the entrance hall.

"Good morning, I'm a prefect. I've been asked to show you

the school. Come with me and I'll take you around." The pupil, one of the upper sixths, led me from the assembly hall. Her manner was gentle, her face seemed the colour of an under-ripe banana and her neatly groomed hair resembled the flesh of over-ripe pumpkin. Hers were the first light grey eyes I'd ever looked at. As soothing as a gentle breeze was the voice of this tour guide.

"This is your locker for your books. You will need a padlock . . . you can choose any desk you wish, but if you're near a window you'll see people coming and going on Carmichael Street . . . This is the cloak room. No. we don't say toilet, we say cloakroom." She spoke Properly and was difficult to understand.

"Which class I in?" I asked in Guianese.

"You're in 3B, the Lower Thirds, and here's the office where you bring money to buy text books. Miss Lall will help you. Up these stairs there's the library . . . it's wonderful . . . of course, we have quite a few magazines in French. That was Miss Broedhagen. She's really outstanding, she'll teach you Art in this studio." I was giddy.

"The Geography room is above the science labs . . . Do you like cooking and sewing? The new Home Ec mistress likes everything in that wing to be as neat as Government House . . . The bike stalls are over there . . . You'll be using the assembly hall for music and PE; you'll have to change into your gym clothes near the costume cupboards behind the drama curtains, backstage, terribly dusty and mouldy . . . That's the sickbay, that's the office of Miss Harris, the Headmistress who welcomed everyone in Assembly. Ummm humm . . . Miss Harris was the white lady with the Dutchboy haircut . . . The staff room and their tea room are here . . ." I was overwhelmed. After one-room Fredericksburg school, the marvel of Bishops!

We passed by, but never commented on, like it did not exist, the servants' quarters under the back stairs. I was aware that one of the women's eyes followed my black presence approvingly.

44

Tall, bulky, dark Dora, the head servant, and I exchanged secret smiles. Was this the beginning of a discreet friendship?

I'd brought no lunch that day and realised that it would be impossible to ride home for a meal and return in time, so I spent half an hour in the cloakroom. Then we sat under the giant tamarind and mahogany trees that shaded the walkways. We promenaded past pink oleander bushes of generous proportion and along the fences of red and orange hibiscus which cloistered us from the outside world.

"That's Paulette Bailey. Her father is Peter Bailey, the Test cricket commentator on radio." Now there's a connection I could understand!

"They are the Gajraj sisters, their family is connected to the motor car importing business downtown. That's Lynne, daughter of Judge Morris. Oh, that's Pamela Vaughn-Cooke, you know, her father is the principal of the Teachers' Training College. Pretty, isn't she? You've heard of Alphonso's record store? That's Jeanette Alphonso. And her? She . . .!" My eyes were already magnetised by that vision. I gazed at the prettiest girl of African descent that I had ever seen in the flesh. Prettier than Lena Horne. She had exquisitely styled, straightened hair, gypsy gold earrings, a well fitted uniform, an expensive wristwatch and the air of a princess who had always been treated like the Queen. Her eyes were luminous, compelling. Her skin walnut brown.

"She's Sandra Williams. Her father, Dr Frank Williams, is one of the few Negro people on our Board of Governors." These girls were the crème de la crème of the nation, in wealth, birth, brains and now beauty. Bishops Girls.

I longed to explain that I was somebody too, to say, "I'm Nelson's grand-daughter. You know, 'Doc' Nelson, the head pharmacist at Mackenzie hospital. He even lives there in one of the white staff cottages in the hospital compound. And my grandmother is Mrs Nelson, who has the only bakery in

Christianburg, across the river from Mackenzie, and ours is the biggest house in the village!"

Of course that would never do. So I lost in that very moment of arrival one of my most precious possessions, my place, my recognition in my community. In Bishops terms I was redefined as poor, black and unknown, all of which were viewed as liabilities.

'Please' and 'Thank you' dropped easily from my lips, as Mummy had drilled me. "Don't shame me when yo go there! Show them at Bishops that yo have home training, yo wasn't dragged up. 'Excuse me please', or 'Pardon me' will take you a long way."

Who could have guessed, however, that I would immediately be a raft adrift in a surging river when the older girls who had acquired it, and the imported English teachers who had brought it here, spoke their Oxbridge-accented Properly to me?

Which is not to deny that the lessons were fabulous and joyful although they felt completely disconnected from my life.

> The birch in the wood is a dancer in green
> With the greenest of skirts that ever was seen.

"What is a birch, please Miss Bacchus?" I asked my bewitchingly well-groomed, petite Music mistress who conducted us in four part choral works. With sweeps of the hand she indicated a note held here, a soft tone there, and seamlessly joined in the other half of the choir. This fooled the ear into believing that the five minute long melody had no pauses for breath. We managed to sound terribly Chapel Royal English.

> Blackberrying time is with us again . . .

> . . . She's singing and swinging and calling for me,
> for the apple-tree fairy is mine. Don't you see!

Did it matter that I knew none of those plants, those seasons, those landscapes? By the end of the year I had begun to make sense of Shakespeare and Wordsworth, their words set as lyrics to densely scored music for massed choirs.

Blow, blow, thou Winter wind,
Thou art not so unkind as man's ingratitude . . .

I wander'd lonely as a cloud
That floats on high o'er vales and hills,
When all at once I saw a crowd,
A host, of golden daffodils;
Beside the lake, beneath the trees,
Fluttering and dancing in the breeze.

History lessons made no personal sense when we studied the Phoenicians, Cretans, Babylonians, Egyptians, or Medes and Persians. Then I ran into my, and Granny Adrianna's, old mates, Abraham, Joshua and David, Solomon and Ezra. I knew I'd study history eagerly after that. Alexander the Great, Pericles, Phidippides, Socrates all flashed past until we came to the Roman Empire at year's end.

"I hope you have enjoyed studying this text, *The Basement*", said Black Guianese Miss Campbell, one History mistress who always managed to lace the blandest, fact-filled lessons with the over-proof rum of compelling storytelling. No wonder I floated out of her classes drunk on ideas and words. Given, however, that we lived in Georgetown where buildings perch safely on stilts, in case the dykes burst and the Atlantic Ocean once again floods our lands, no basements existed. It took a good five years and a Canadian pen-pal before I saw the connection between the title of my history text, *The Basement*, and the early Middle Eastern empires we had studied.

The most delicious madness infected me when I discovered words. I felt I'd become a Kankawa kite, flyyyyiiiinnggg . . . all six metres of my streaming colour-drenched tail dancing just below the heavens in a lively Easter-Monday-holiday breeze. I read voraciously, indiscriminately, not always understanding the world within those books. There was *School Girl's Annual, Elle* and *Paris Match* after my first year of French, *Dickens, Courier* and *Punch, The Daily Chronicle* newspaper, *The Times* of London, de la Mare, Rossetti, Spender, Joyce, Austin, encyclopaedias, comics, fairy tales, Kipling, books on the Royal Family. Where were Guianese novels and stories for the reading, I wondered. Homework left unfinished, earned poor marks.

". . . because the three books were due back in the school library by midday, Miss." So I joined the American Embassy library on High Street where the illustrated volumes revealed in those photographs a world of wealth for ordinary people, or so it seemed. A wealth I never imagined for common folks. One or two photographs even showed black people. Moreover, if I were desperate for cookery, sewing or craft books there were volumes in the Carnegie library on the corner of High Street, in front of the Cenotaph. Then I took to browsing for hours in bookshops and arriving home late to a telling off.

Whenever my life in that Paris apartment with a view of the Eiffel Tower became too hectic, . . . my dear, all that shopping at Balenciaga's! . . . I'd drive away in my Jaguar from *Courier* magazine, to the Viscount aeroplane bound for Britain. Sitting on the familiar tartan blanket in the Lakes District hours later, I'd look beyond my Harrods' hamper packed with picnic fare from Fortnum and Mason's to admire, what else . . . a host of golden daffodils! Ahhh . . . dusk in my stately home on this side of the Channel. Time to slip into the pearl encrusted taffeta and lace ball gown, satin shoes, elbow length gloves . . . no, no . . . the tiara is too . . . too . . . the three strand Queen Mary style pearl choker against my dark skin will do ever so nicely . . . for my presentation to Princess Margaret (I preferred her), at Buckingham Palace.

"Mona, we're waiting for you to begin translating from *Elle fondit en larme*. Never mind the commotion on Carmichael Street." The French Mistress struggled to keep her tone pleasant.

"Get up and wash de blasted wares!" Mummy roughed me out of sleep and bed late one night. "Who you think yo are?" Mummy had come one holiday to visit us at Danny Boy's, where we were being boarded during my first year at Bishops. As none of us, Mummy included, had been taught, knew how to, nor liked cooking, we all shirked it and made a big show of the cleaning tasks we undertook. Out into the fog I stumbled to the yard pump for a bucket of cold well water and arrived back into the cold kitchen, crying, unco-ordinated, angry and grumbling quietly. Fumbling fingers lit the kerosene lamp with the fourth match. Cold hands poured the cold water into the enamel washing-up basin then rubbed the dishcloth with sunlight soap. Soapy palms picked up the first object and "CRRASHH"! The Royal Albert porcelain teapot imported from England by Mummy's parents, that representation of all of my mother's finer aspirations, lay in fragments on the dark kitchen floor—its white innards in death tremors.

My mother bounded out, snatched up and raised a length of fire wood. Unwilling to distinguish between a lack of co-ordination and an act of anger by me, since the effect on the teapot was exactly the same, she refused to listen and thrashed me till exhaustion stopped her, sweating, speechless and breathless.

Our lodgings in Sandy Babb St, Kitty, a district of Georgetown, were one large room at the rear of a small grocery store owned by Danny Boy. Our beds and table were behind a curtain. Cooking was done in an attached, smoke-blackened kitchen with chopped wood stored in a raised fireplace. The village shower was an outdoor corrugated, galvanised-iron cubicle. The toilet, into which the houses behind our building also tipped

49

chamber pots, was another cubicle over a septic tank, its toilet bowl missing the wooden seat.

Dinah with one glass eye, and two other women, one middle aged, one a teenager, with little interest in either the shop or us, were to care for us. Their time was spent in a bougainvillea covered, wooden cottage up the train-line that ran from Georgetown to Buxton. On a rare occasion I was taken to visit that house, where I observed their job, with eyes the size of pot lids. They and Danny Boy were helping a client rid himself of his demons by applying head pressure to the seated man's stomach. For that service and for the forecasting of a favourable future the company of four earned a fee far greater than their grocery store's profits for a week.

Danny Boy, stiff of movement, spittle-spraying of speech, fiftyish, miracle-man, 'see-far-ian' and small storeowner, exerted a resented influence over his three women helpers. We rarely saw Danny Boy, which was a blessing in its own kind of way. In popular language he was an 'obeah man', one who practised spirit-magic.

What good would it do to ask Mummy for a place elsewhere to live? She hadn't listened once before. How could I convey the unease, confide my feeling that this place was both evil and violent to live in?

Eight

Like a prayer, I recounted my wanderings. "Sent away at seven to board with Aunt Carrie . . . moved to dear Aunt Lydia Maud's . . . moved back to Christianburg to live at both Mudsie's home and Mummy's new bedsitter at Mackenzie opposite the Catholic Church . . . sent to Wakenaam . . . boarded at Danny Boy's . . . five shifts in six years. Now where next shall I wander like Moses in the desert?" Such effort in search of the Promised Land of a Bishops education. Mind you, this secret monologue of mine, and it had to be secret, was mouthed in Bishops Properly. I was fascinated and amused at the 'how they speak in the pictures' sound of my voice, an accent Claire and Keith mimicked and laughed at as being 'like an English duck'. Guianese who spoke that way in public were cut about with the most unkindest put-down. "You trying to be white, talking like dat!"

The answer to my question came to me.

"Don't pay de fool round me!" fumed stick-thin, arthritic, bent-backwards Granny Adrianna, when she arrived to care for us at a new address on Durban Street. Situated a kilometre away from where I'd once lived at dear Aunt Lydia Maud's, Mummy had moved us into this Georgetown apartment and returned upriver to teach. We were jubilant. Old Granny Adrianna's bark was all she had. No bite, she was like a toothless she-wolf sent to suckle us, her great-grand children. That we called our great-grandmother 'Granny' never seemed strange to us. That was the name our mother used, so we used it too.

"Go today and pay Khailan dis rent money. That East Indian landlord would put you out in de street if yo is only one day late wid de rent!"

"Yes Granny!" we'd sing out and do the errands, wondering if what she said were true.

"Eat up! You'se a boy child. Yo can't grow meagre and weak!" she'd scold Keith, piling more servings of coconut rice and curried arapima fish on his plate, while stroking his head.

"Among-you is to sit down right now and do yo homework. Yo-all can't grow duncey, or people in de world will ride yo likka donkey! And yo Mona, when yo finished yo Latin yo is to read dis chapter from First Samuel in dis Bible with de big print; read it to me. Yo boy, don't fall asleep over yo homework! Yo sitting scholarship soon."

Seated cosily under the amazing electric lights, we'd study then talk like family around the square dining table.

"Is where me father living, Granny?" I asked one evening as she taught me to patch the seat on Keith's khaki pants.

"What stupid-ness yo askin me? Yo is to ask yo mother about dat!"

"But, I want to know now. I ent gun see Mummy till . . ."

"Well don't bother-out me with yo asking!" she snapped, but her sharp manner never put me off because I knew Granny Adrianna liked me.

"Is just dat Joy Best does always say, 'Mummy and Daddy' and I never hear me-self say dat." How do I tell the rest, I wondered?

"And Cicely Rodway was walking down Brickdam to school wid me yesterday and she say that I come from a broken home. And I say 'Is why you talking such stupid-ness.' And she said, 'This is sensible-ness. And I really sorry for you, but you do come from a broken home because you father don't live wid you-all.'"

"And who de France ask she opinion in the first place?" Claire burst in heatedly.

"Some people should give they mouth midnight-rest!" Granny Adrianna sizzled.

"I just had to tell she Ciceley Rodway that me home ent got a single crack in any o' the walls. So I ent come from no broken home at all!" I spoke emphatically.

"Good! Yo got a plaster fo every sore! Yo is to tend to she in future!"

"Tell she to kiss your ribs," advised Keith, who rarely joined in. Granny Adrianna back-patted and over-saw my darning. But I could see from her ink-eyes, her knowing-eyes, that she was thinking.

Reading the bible aloud gave me the chance to experiment with 'that sound'. It had enchanted me whenever Mrs Potter read *The Wind in the Willows* to our class at Bishops because she knew some of us were slow readers. She magic-carpeted us through the chapters of David Copperfield, the class chuckling at her declaring, "Barkis is willing!"

"Yo reads clear bout Hannah and old Eli; yo says de words really nice," Granny Adrianna praised me. Soon I was reading my books to Granny Adrianna with the intonation of a selection of my English mistresses.

I had by now, in the Upper Thirds, begun to train for and to enter the annual national elocution contests and singing competitions in which Bishops pupils took the top prizes.

Like giant brooms, the palm trees
Sweep the stardust from the dreaming skies,
As through half-opened door of sleep
Bird carols of the morning riiiseee!

My voice would crescendo. Had I learnt it accurately? Then I would have to practice the more serious John Donne set piece:

Death, be not proud, though some have called thee
Mighty and dreadful, for thou art not so . . .

Six weeks later it was clear to me that my classmates' admiration
of my recitation rehearsals had nothing to do with how well
I had mastered the skills of public speaking. They admired how
much of England my colonial voice echoed and evoked. Ah well,
with hours of practice, the nerve 'to talk likka dem Backra people'
in public, and the appearance that was the result of impeccable
grooming on the contest day, I came away from the stage at
Queen's College elated. I'd won a first prize in the under-fourteen
section for poetry recitation and third prize as a soloist in singing.
This seemed quite a feather in my cap given that many of the
contestants there were English born. Furthermore, our choir,
in which I sang soprano, won first prizes in two sections. One
was a complex, soaring difficult tone poem, praising the beauty
of Guiana. It had been specially composed for the festival by a
Guianese. The other, 'Buttercup', was English hedgerows and
hedgehogs to the core.

There was little feeling of my being the conquering girl
warrior, returning home with trophies. Everyone looked blankly
at those blue and white certificates on which my name was
printed in black. They didn't understand what those meant as
they hadn't seen me perform. With every success I yearned to
show my Bishops knowledge to the family, my science log book
with test-tubes, bunsen burners, magnets and pipettes to someone
who would admire my efforts. Claire's High School lacked the
facilities to teach everyone science and her French did not allow
her an understanding of my French carolling. The arabesques
constructed with precision using compasses, in geometry class,
were merely pretty to my sister and brother. Not mathematical
achievements, just pretty shapes. But Mudsie, my Mummy's
mother, she'd always understood. Mudsie away down river at
Christianburg.

I remembered one day as a five year old when the world had seemed sapphire bright. I'd emerged from the Christianburg schoolhouse into an oven-hot, equatorial noon, and eyed the blue skies overhead and the road home. A sheet of pelting, grey, coarse-drop rain sat squarely between where my midday meal awaited and where I stood. Without a raincoat, there was still no hesitation. The writing slate would have to sit atop my oiled and plaited hair, to keep at least my head warm-dry. My Royal Reader book was placed atop the slate and I dashed most of the way home feeling warm sky-drops peppering my body like grape shot. Bounding into Mudsie's pie-scented bread shop and whipping off the wet reading book I announced, "Home Mudsie! Look, nuh Mudsie? Miss Carr gave me stars fo all o' me sums this morning. I save it from the rain fo show you."

Mudsie looked at the teacher's chalk ticks at the side of my writing, beamed approval, cut a slice of cassava and raisin pone and gave it to me with a flourish, then said, "Nice, you got everything right. Good picknee, good. Eat this. Only, next time don't put the book where it can get wet. It only make of paper so it will fall to pieces . . . and keep working at yo studies. Good girl." Then she disappeared into the bakery to push loaves of bread, balanced on her long wooden peel, into the giant concrete oven.

The world felt dry-warm, although I stood there drenched to the skin.

The delight of finding out that 'agricola' in Latin, meant a farmer, helped me to make sense of a place like Agricola village plantation a distance away from Georgetown. Sharing this and giving Granny Adrianna a recital of the anthem 'Thanks Be To God' which Miss Bacchus was teaching us, encouraged Granny Adrianna's questions.

"Is where you will sing this anthem?"

"At St George's Cathedral."

"When and why?" she wished to know.

"Two Sundays from now. For Commemoration service. It's to remember all the Old Girls, the Headmistresses and teachers. They built up Bishops. The Governor-General will be there. The Dean will conduct the service and . . ."

"Your mother won't mind you going?" Granny Adrianna said. I thought that was an odd remark, but didn't wish to break the mood of the moment to question and perhaps argue. Which was as well, for our harmony led to Granny Adrianna's confiding, "I know Latin. Can sing in Latin, yo know. The whole Catholic Mass."

"True, Granny Adrianna?" I asked. "How come you know that?"

"Well I grew up wid some Putagee people . . ."

"Portuguese people" I corrected.

". . . that me mother put me wid. Mama-Sarah did just come over with me brother and me from Barbados. Round 1880. Left her husband for good and come over on a sloop . . . hadn't relatives here. So she took a fish stall in Big Market . . ."

"Stabroek Market," I corrected.

". . . and she pay them people fo look after me. They was Catholics, and I learnt the Gloria, the Kyrie, the Sanctus . . ."

"Can you sing them for me? Teach me?" I asked, unable to credit that this old lady with the standard three education knew Latin.

When Granny Adrianna lifted up her voice and sang words and melodies learnt as an eight year old, the notes were true, the voice pure, the words flawlessly pronounced. I felt awe and admiration for this woman who seemed to hold continuous surprises. This old woman I knew earliest as the thin one with cold feet, who smelled of coconut oil and Cusson's talcum powder, who kidnapped me as a wee child to sleep in her bed and hugged me all night long as her hot water-bottle.

"Teach me the Gloria," I begged, and thus was forged a bond

of song between us. Almost every night I would add, "Granny, what it was like coming as a picknee from Barbados?"

"Granny, what your first husband was like, Mr Wickham?"

"Why did you mother marry you off at my age, fourteen?"

"Why was it special to celebrate Queen Victoria's Jubilee?"

"Granny, how your son David, died?"

"Why you stop living with your second husband, Mr James, Granny?"

"How come you made enough money by yourself to buy a house in Worthmanville? In the 1920s at dat?"

"I couldn't bring up five children on my own Granny, so, how you do it with only clothes-washing money?" My store of questions was bottomless.

"You too fast! Asking too much questions!" she'd snap. All the same, days later she'd tell me her stories as we sewed, and in a round about way would answer my questions.

"Claire and I lived with a Catholic too, Granny Adrianna. That was Aunt Carrie." I said. "She took us to Mass at Brickdam Cathedral." But as Granny Adrianna said nothing I changed the subject.

". . . and do you believe in Jumbies, and Come-Back spirits, and the Holy Ghost and Water-People and . . .?" I asked all ears and eyes. A harsh snort told me that Granny Adrianna was particularly itchy about this topic, as if she were wearing loofa knickers.

"I don't believe in all o' this foolishness and 'working obeah'; and paying money to Palla-Walla people from the French West Indies fo 'see far'; and making spells with white candles and white cloth," her words were drenched with anger. But why?

"And I don't believe neither in Backoo-spirit-voices and high wine and white roosters and rose water and incense. It's a whole lot o' bewitchment and foolishness to me!"

"But Granny, you just sang about the Holy Ghost, in Latin," I argued.

57

"That's God's Religion. That's different. That's holy!" Granny Adrianna insisted. "But I wants no foolishness round me! Remember King Saul!"

". . . and the witch of Endor . . . yes . . . but then, tell me this," I'd say, enjoying the verbal tussle and asking another question to provoke discussion.

Granny Adrianna cared for us, Claire seemed to enjoy life at Central High School, I enjoyed Bishops, and Keith sat his scholarship exam.

However enjoyable her company was for me, life in the city for Granny Adrianna meant being cut off from her Brethren Church sisters, her river, her other daughters, Gladys and Iris, and their families, and the gossip about the villagers which one heard in the market from the 'spit-press'. Polishing Khailan's floors, cooking for us, washing and ironing day in day out were hardly her idea of paradise. I wished I could have seen the future. Great Aunt Iris, the youngest of Granny Adrianna's children, wrote to Mummy:

> Dear Clarene,
>
> How are you? . . . Its time you learn to bring up your children yourself. How old are you now? Thirty-five? You taking advantage! Our Mother is an old woman of seventy and she has got no business minding your three teenager picknee. They are her great-grands! What you think it is at all? You trying to kill the old woman or what? . . .
>
> Yours,
> Auntie Iris.

Granny Adrianna prepared to leave for Christianburg at the end of the term.

Attending a Bishops party for all one hundred girls belonging to 'Victoria House' was an enjoyable diversion.

Girls in the school were assigned to one of five teams, called

Houses. Each House was named after an English queen or past English headmistress. Costumed as elephants, ghosts and jugglers we went on a mystery-tour of the backstage of the auditorium. In the pitch dark, pelted with ice, we panicked as if ghost-struck.

Later, ever so delicately we ate English tea-cakes we had brought, sipped an English tea I had never before tasted and sang campfire songs from America.

It was also during that party that a House Mistress invited me to consider joining the school's junior debating team as a second speaker. The contest against St Roses Ursaline Convent was in three weeks. The Motion: 'That city life is superior to country life'. It was a wonderful opportunity to make friends and to learn teamwork, as well as to practice speaking Pproperly in public for an evening, without fear of criticism. Rehearsing before groups of housemates and classmates helped me to sharpen my thinking. The debate, however, made little sense to me because in British Guiana there were not very sharp differences between country and city life as there were in England, where I believe the topic had been thought up. Hadn't I won scholarship from a country school? Hadn't Wakenaam been wonderful?

Nervous but controlled, we of the Proposition worked as an excellent team on the night and won. The debate, with our names, was reported in the Georgetown newspaper. Our arguments championing city life made no difference to Granny's life at home; she sailed from the city for Christianburg.

Sometimes ah feel like a motherless child,
A long way from hoooooooom.
A long wayyyyyyyys from home!

I sang and cried in my dark bedroom after her departure. Claire and Keith were like rudderless ships.

"Hello, I'm Mona, from the row behind you. What's your

name?" I asked of a pretty newly arrived pupil with teeth which slanted a tiny bit inwards. She was vivacious, had an open smile, light brown hair and a back which seemed somewhat curved.

"Janet Jones. My parents are from Britain, but we've lived in Jinja, Kampala and Entebbe for a few years. We'll be in BG for three years or so," she spoke engagingly.

"You'll like it here. Did you have to pass a hard exam to come into Bishops?" I wished to know.

"Oh no. I just had an interview, and that wasn't difficult. But not any sort of an exam. We don't have to sit an exam if we're white," she said charmingly.

"Whaaaat?" I raged, sounding not unlike Mr McGowan. Janet jumped. My classmates looked sideways at me, said nothing but scattered. "Is not fair. You are not even Guianese and you can come here without sitting anything. But we . . . I had to fight the whole nation for a place at Bishops." Too angry to speak quietly my voice seemingly gushed up from an unstoppable volcano.

"How dare you! From England to boot! My grandmother pays the taxes for this school! And you can get into Bishops easily! Without . . ."

"It will not do, my girl, to behave like a fishwife in the corridor! You have one detention for making a commotion!" a French mistress said discreetly, sweeping past me on her way to the staffroom. She had given me my first detention.

Nine

"Where will we board?" I had asked after Granny Adrianna had left. Then I felt them again. Heart hammers I'd called them, from that first time as a nine year old when I'd noticed them.

Claire and I had been happily boarding in 1952 in Georgetown with Aunt Lydia Maud. In what was then a daily after school routine, I'd ridden with Claire to the red public phone booth opposite Bourda Market. Lifting the receiver, like magic, a human voice crooned, "Number please". Never having used a phone, knowing nobody who owned one, possessing neither number nor money nor even a clue to the words one spoke into the black round metal mouthpiece, I'd let fly a string of phrases to fry your ear tubes. Clang! The receiver would slam into the cradle. Yaaah! The shriek as I bolted. Claire frowned on my escapade.

That afternoon as I'd pushed the door to bolt from the booth a large wheel was inches from my body and on the bicycle silhouetted against a bright sky, sat a burly, black, uniformed policeman reaching forward to grab me. Dodging, ducking, I'd scampered to Claire who was holding my bike and we'd torn off home as if dark night jumbies were pursuing us. The heart hammers nearly killed me.

However, heart hammers, like bends in the river, are different from each other. I remember the time a spider monkey I'd often teased at the Georgetown zoo reached through the bars when I wasn't looking, yanked off and Tarzan-ed away with my vivid red-plaid hair ribbon, "Had he grabbed my hair! My!" I thought, almost fainting from the heart hammers! The knocking knees! The feeling of being a dugout canoe tossing over swirling eddies.

"Claire! Come quick! Dey comin'" I had called out across Aunt Lydia Maud's dining room. Together we'd shared an open, second storey window, inspecting the Saturday afternoon parades below Aunt Lydia Maud's front picket fence at the corner of Durban and Cemetery Roads. Aunt Lydia Maud would either be ironing the family's clothes or preparing to cook dinner by picking the rice to remove all discoloured grains. How different from life in Aunt Carrie's formal, wealthy, Edwardian mansion was that year boarding at Aunt Lydia Maud's.

To nine and ten year old eyes the pageants below were fabulous, absorbing, a fairy kingdom come alive. There were uniformed brass bands, black horse drawn carriages with a black suited, top hatted coachman and well dressed men and women seated within. Occasionally we saw a landau. Sometimes the foot procession took twenty minutes to troop by while we gave a commentary.

"De women dress nice, eh? Dey all got on green skirts."

"Everyone wearing white aprons."

". . . and fancy hats with sprays of flowers, cocked on their heads."

"And green leaves between their lips . . ."

"and white gloves . . ."

"but dey walking with one hand behind their back."

". . . is why, Dear Aunt?"

Aunt Lydia Maud would join our lookout then decipher the spectacle.

"Oh, dey belongs to de Foresters' Lodge. Dis is de Grand Lodge Master's funeral." Or, "He was one o' de big shots in de Trades Union Council. De long-shoremen giving he a wonderful send off." Or ". . . dey is Garveyites, Marcus Garvey followers."

Then the heart hammers would pummel me. Four sleek, perfectly groomed horses with shiny tack would prance into view pulling a high-mounted glass walled coach in which lay the elaborate, solitary casket of polished wood and bright brass trim. Ooh! The circular colourful wreaths. The crunching sounds of hundreds of feet and dozens of carriage wheels. Those noises were the aural tribute of our people accompanying each African descendant to his or her final resting place at Le Repentir Cemetery. Fascination with these dramatic processions was like a broad, windswept stretch in a wave-dancing river.

So, after Granny left us I wondered where and with whom we would now live. Aunt Lydia Maud was long dead and her house sold. Mummy, as an only child, had no aunties or uncles for us on her side. Despite there being five of Dad's brothers and sisters, and Dad's mother living in Georgetown, we knew we couldn't turn to them. We hadn't kept in touch with my father's kin. Years before, Aunt Lydia Maud had written Mummy to say:

Dear Clarene,

How are you? I hope fine with God's blessing.

I wanted to give you a hand by keeping Claire and Mona to board with me. After all the girls is my nephew Edmund's children just as much as they is your own. But I belongs to Edmund's side of the family. Seeing that you and your husband left and you not even talking to one another, it make life hard for me. I have to study the feelings of my side of the family too. Keeping your children here in my home is getting me in bad with my own brothers and sisters. And with their children too. I don't want bad feelings in my house. And things between our two families is not peaceful.

As you know I always says: 'peace is plenty'. So I have to ask you to please come and take Claire and Mona to live with you. Please come now.

God bless you.

Your loving

Dear Aunt Lydia Maud.

In response Mummy materialised out of nowhere, as once before. Taking us away this time, unlike our leaving Aunt Carrie's, was devastating because Claire and I were unaware of the letter which had been sent. We had enjoyed Aunt Lydia Maud's cooking, this light-brown, gigantic woman's gentleness, her warm mansion-size house, and within it the fourteen of our relatives living together. We had had cousins to play with, aunties to comb our knotty hair, policemen great uncles to tell us stories of arresting burglars; breadfruit and coconuts aplenty and cherry, soursop, ghynep and starapple trees to feast from. The latest gossip floated up from Mr Dooley's butcher shop below Auntie Ann's apartment in one part of the house and drifted out the door of Cousin Gwen's beauty parlour which was situated by the front door.

The only wreck in the river had been an uncle who took to feeling over our flat chests, but I'd told on him to Aunt Lydia Maud and to his wife Auntie . . . and he had immediately stopped doing that to Claire and me. No one ever told Mummy about this incident, not even Claire nor I, I suppose because it was no longer occurring. So we three mystified females, wondering exactly why Claire and I had been told to leave, sailed home. On our joyless steamer trudge to Christianburg the heart hammers were hard, dull, slow, like navigating 'gainst tide in a strong current on a pitch black night.

I went on to live two years at home, moving easily between Mudsie's house and Mummy's new bedsitter across the river at Mackenzie near to the Catholic Church. I remember that time best from a calypso we sang about the West Indies defeating the MCC at Lords, for the very first time. King George even went to see a day's play:

Cricket, lovely Cricket. At Lords where I saw it.
Yardley tried his best but Goddard won the test.
Cricket, 'e got plenty fun,
Second Test de West Indies won!
With those little pals of mine
Rahmadin and Valentine!

The West Indians had invaded the cricket pitch with steel drums and dance, at the end of the test match. This caused the BBC commentator to describe their behaviour as, "A little too much of a good thing!" Everyone used that phrase to death, speaking in a pluty English accent, then collapsing with laughter.

The following year, 1953, I marched to the cinema with pupils of my primary school to see 'A Queen is Crowned', and marvelled at the sight of Queen Elizabeth wobbling slightly, for an instant, as the heavy crown was placed on her young head. It was after that lovely homestay that I'd next journeyed to study for scholarship at Wakenaam.

Now, years on in early '57, with Granny returned to Christianburg, I was desperate.

"If there is no one to take care of us will I have to sail home again?" I pondered. More was at stake this time around, as leaving the capital would mean forfeiting hard won Bishops.

"Halt!" the man's voice commanded. "Halt this minute!" Claire and I froze. A warm stream spurted down and burned its way along my trembling leg and ankle.

"Drop what you carrying!" Claire and I flung the bundles from our heads on to the roadside. His torch shone over my mattress, clothing, bookbag, school shoes and uniform, then on to Claire's knotted sheet from which bulged pots, books, crockery and cutlery.

"What you got dere?" he snapped, shining the torch over our thirteen and fourteen year old frames covered in old clothes. The beam swept back over the jumble.

"Is we own things," Claire answered softly.

"Open de bundle leh me see." Claire's shaking fingers complied. He saw her exercise books with Central High School on the cover.

"And where you girls going to dis hour o' de night? Is nearly midnight!" he spoke sternly.

The street lights were far off and because he was as black skinned as we were and dressed in his black serge police uniform we couldn't even make out his features. Just the torch beam dancing on the spokes of his bicycle wheel on the grass verge. Heart hammers! They belted my eardrums. Thudded my skull. Voice deserted me. Tears surged down my nose.

"We movin'," Claire spoke. "We goin' to a new house."

"Where you movin' from?"

"Khailan place. Up de road dere," Claire pointed.

"Where you father? He somewhere here? He in charge o' de movin'?"

"We ent got a father," Claire said. "We father . . . not here."

"Well den, where your mother is?" he persisted, torch full into our faces. The debater and winner of poetry prizes could find no voice but Claire was saying, "Me mother gone back to Christianburg. She pay for dis place and she tell us to move." Claire was panting and near to tears. "We only got dese few things more to carry . . ." Claire looked like a frightened rabbit dazzled by car lights.

"Well why you didn't move you things in daylight? Is dangerous. Two girl children . . . dis hour o de night . . . out on de road like dis."

Neither of us could have explained how humiliated we would have felt to have packed our paltry goods, to have hoisted all on to our heads like expedition porters, and to have shifted in full public view. Mummy had had no money to waste on a donkey cart to shift a mere block away. We stood mute.

"All right. Tie up back you bundle and hoist up back you

66

things. You got far to go?" his voice sounded less stern, even fatherly.

"We was just goin' to turn in here. Mr Thorne's yard. Dis is we new house." Claire's quiet voice was quavering now.

"Well, I gun come to mek sure you all safe." he said.

I was suspicious but it was all right. He saw us into the yard and left after we had bolted ourselves inside the back door.

We fell down there and then on my mattress shaking and crying. Keith, who had been waiting for us in the house, asked, "Is wha' happened?"

How could I quieten the heart hammers to explain to this exquisitely innocent eleven year old that I'd felt like a canoeist careening midstream on a swift river current, to within a few yards of the lip of a waterfall?

Fending for ourselves through six weeks' wait for a new housekeeper was surprisingly pleasant. We shopped carefully and I cooked what I had learnt in Home Economics at Bishops and from Granny. Claire and Keith told me that their favourites were cook-up rice, split pea soup, curried groper with roti and bakes with fried salted codfish. Claire and I made the house firebright with brushes and soapy water, floor polish and dusting cloths. We girls washed clothes the way Granny and I had done at the river and I patched Keith's pants as Granny had shown me at the square dining table.

One evening some friends visiting the capital from Claire's old Eccles High School in Mackenzie, came by and in spite of our having no food to share with them, they plugged in a radio they'd brought to hear the Saturday evening hour long record hit parade. Then, on Mr Thorne's concrete yard, in the orange sunset of a warm Guiana evening, the boys displayed wild flips, angular shuffles, bold jumps in the air, strong kicks, fast spins and energetic drops to the ground into splits!

Their shirts became wet, foreheads sprinkled sweat. Arms flung the girls out, sideways, around, up, across their backs. Hands pulled the pretty partners through their legs with swift wild strength. The girls, wide skirted in stiff frilly petticoats, nimble footed and flat shoed, billowed from one hand hold to another. They did everything in perfect rhythm with the music. The air was afire with carefree laughter, shrieks and loud music. It vibrated with youthful energy, rustling skirts and jiving feet.

Someone on the hit parade scream-sang:

> Whap baba looba
> Ba lop bam boo!
> Tutti frutti ah da looty!

The Radio Demerara announcer proclaimed his name as Little Richard and the boys told Claire that this raging style was the new black American dance craze called Rock-n'-Roll.

Claire and I joined in with shy, awkward enthusiasm. Keith stared mesmerised. This bigger thrill than zegging, these new dance movements became part of my body memory. And those heart hammers gusted me to the skies the way river mist ascends; swaying, floating, soaring upwards at the touch of the fierce mid-morning sun.

"I don't like her!" I confided to Claire at my first glimpse of Olivia alighting from the taxi. She was a short, round, unsmiling, thirtyish woman with pouting lips.

"You always!" Claire chided, quietly furious. "Mummy trying hard fo get somebody fo us and all you doin' is complainin'! Scthoops!" she sucked her teeth in disgust and went to help Olivia with the bags.

Two daughters, Junia, a thin brown fawn of a three year old and Judith, a round bouncing, curly-haired, chatty two year old accompanied Olivia. They settled into the smaller bedroom while we three siblings shared the larger. The all-in-one kitchen, dining, shower-booth were at the back end of the flat and became Olivia's domain where we ventured to eat or shower but not to socialise. We didn't feel that welcome.

The bedrooms and a passageway were in the middle of the flat and the front end had a living room area, graced by a couch with only three good legs as the sole stick of furniture. We sat on the polished floor when trying to write our homework. Within a week Olivia said. "Your mother's money not sufficient to feed you-all. I had was fo spend eighty cents o' me own money fo buy flour this week." We dis-believed her, having kept house ourselves for six weeks and not having had a belly-rumbling-hungry-day. We were not being fed as well by Olivia as we had fed ourselves, but we dared not challenge her.

Two weeks later she wrote to Mummy.

Dear Clarene,
　　Greetings. I received the basket you send last Saturday by Mr Oxley's launch. The girls brought it home safely on a borrowed bike.
　　I want to ask you . . . did you send the coconut cakes for me or was that for your children? And the cassava pone and pumpkins? I wasn't sure. Thanks for the loaves of aniseed bread and the meringue pie that Mudsie baked. We all ate that delicious food by Sunday. Your Mudsie certainly understands she-self in front of an oven, nuh?
　　I noticed that you send washing soaps, blue, starch and shoe polish but I did not know if I could make use of those too. Were they only for your children? Also, your money does not meet to pay for everything, so I had was to take the children's pocket money you send, to make up the difference. I'm trying my best.
　　We are well at this end, praise God. Greetings to you and Mudsie.

Regards,
Olivia

Years later I would learn that Mudsie had read the letter and announced heatedly, "Dis woman so exact. Good Lord. She ent got no peace. Why she can't share everything with everbody and be done wid dat? She got fo WRITE fo ask me who I send starch fo? I can see me and she gun come wrong over dis basket. So before she and me mouth meet ah not sending another blasted thing to Georgetown. Good Lord!"

Knowing nothing of Olivia's letter it had seemed that there was an abrupt end to a practice we'd enjoyed since the days at Aunt Lydia Maud; that of cycling to Water Street wharf, collecting the roomy, cane basket weekly and returning the empty one at the same time to the launch owner. Mudsie collected the empty basket at the Christianburg end. The 'progs' within always included an encouraging letter with no bad family news, penned in Mummy's elegant cursive; Mudsie's cakes, breads, pies, bottled gooseberry and guava jams and Mummy's home made sweets. Mummy often added the clothes she'd sewn for us and Granny donated vegetables reaped from her secret farm on Crown land.

What else? Mudsie's ripe yard-fruits sent according to the seasons; hands of bananas, purple skinned avocadoes, pale green granadillas, yellow papayas and water coconuts. Delicate paper packets hid anything we'd asked for, whether they were stick pens, hair ribbons, Yardley's Lavender talc, needles and threads, vaseline for combing our knotty hair smoothly, or stationery. And of course, the first things we devoured were Mudsie's home made peppermint chunks wrapped in greaseproof paper. Then we'd count our two pennies pocket money each. Now our weekly dose of spoiling had vanished.

Immediately sandwiches and cakes ceased from our bookbags. Along with the peanut bottle full of cold milkless porridge I took to school, I now ate the leaves of the tamarind trees by the tennis court for lunch. Olivia grew noticably plumper and by the end of the term my gold bangles and Claire's gold earrings had disappeared.

Ten

One way our family had of creating a good mood was to pose riddles. I riddled with Keith and sometimes with Bishops friends. I'd say: "Mi-riddle, Mi-riddle, Mi-reee. Me father had a tree . . . What makes you rum-drunk without drinking? Makes you 'dance-through-the-night' happy without dancing? You give up? The School holidays! Yaaaah!"

It seemed everyone wanted more holidays in the mid 1950s. Politicians told the British Government that it was not enough to have Easter, Christmas, Empire Day and August 1st, which celebrates the 1838 proclamation to end the horrific slavery of Africans in British Guiana. As this was the "Land of the Six Peoples" the politicians insisted that we also needed these national holidays: Chinese New Year, the Hindu Festivals of Phagwa and Dewali; and the Muslim Festivals of Eid ul Azha and Eid Mubarrak. Perhaps Corpus Christi would be fitting for the citizens of Portuguese descent, who, apart from the rare exception, were Catholics. An Amerindian Festival to honour the indigenous Guiana Indian tribes was proposed but what it should be called no one knew. The nation thought so little of the Amerindians that we were taught near enough to nothing about them in school, even though invaders from Britain and Europe had come to live in their land since the 1560s.

However, during the holidays we forgot our guardian and our troubles. Mummy was with us. Together we four ambled at night in the capital at Christmas time, buying West Indian golden apples with savoury salt, or tamarinds with pepper garnish from the pavement sellers. We chatted, munching parched peanuts from newspaper packets or gobbling boiled garbanzo beans wrapped in greaseproof paper. Each of us savoured our quarter of an expensive red Canadian apple, (who could have afforded more than one?) and all of us drooled over the Bookers' shop displays.

"Oh Laws! Dat frock material got me in a mass o' confusion!"

"It niiiicccee, so till! Golds, and reds and browns."

"Oh Migawd, de shoes dere, wid de buckle, de black and white one."

"Almighty! Is why you reminding me o' the Tenth Commandment? You don't see from yo seat up in Heaven that these white store people down here *want* me to covet dat lil stove in de show case?" We collapsed laughing at Mummy.

"I wouldn't say, 'No' to that Raleigh bike," Keith resumed.

"Neither me." I'd back him up and we'd be off at it again.

"I'd love a fridge likka dat, not big . . ."

"Lawd! Lokka the Christmas lights! Light bulbs all over de show. De Town Hall! Every side, every tower, every window, all over de wrought-iron 'ginger bread'. Lights dazzling likka Diamond Town!" But we had no money to really shop, nor did it matter.

"Keith!" I once called to him.

"Mi-riddle, mi-riddle, mi-ree. Me Father had a tree . . . What makes the world look like it ent got no limit?"

"When you look up at the sky," he ventured.

"Nah," I contradicted. Then I shared my answer.

For me it was looking as far away as I could, to that blue-brown line which stretches to forever, outreaches to Elsewhere. For me it was squinting at that private spot where the Great Sky Spirit lowers his manly body over Water Mama, his wife.

The horizon skeined across our vast Atlantic Ocean. I found Forever in seascapes rather than in eye-sweeping the arched skyway.

I'm utterly safe, standing on the Georgetown sea-walls. Mummy, Keith and Claire below, are ankle deep in the Demerara silt of the mudflats. The tide is out and a brisk breeze fans me a break-wind of rank mud smell. We females have our skirts hiked up to keep the hems clean. The ocean is prevented from invading the city of Georgetown by this stone wall I'm standing on and by these groynes — a series of stone piers jutting into the ocean at right angles from the sea wall. It's the August holidays and I feel expansive, heady, as large as the world.

"Hey Keithy-Beaty, catch that crab before it runs into the mud hole nuh? EEEH!"

"I caught one! I got . . . EEH! It pinched me!"

"Drop it in me skirt!"

"Ha ha! Claire's shins . . . they muddy like if she went to crab dance!"

"You got something I could eat, please Mummy?"

"Can we take a lil dip Mummy? It safe here . . ."

"Too muddy! But have a race," Mummy would invite. "You-all race from this groyne to that one and come back, for a peanut brittle. Ready? On your marks! Get set! Go!"

Jumping from the sea-wall, thin as a wire, I outsprint heavy Claire and bow-legged Keith, kicking up mud showers in my wake, barrelling with a feeling of exhilaration, the bracing Atlantic salt breeze caressing my face and chest. But my heart dies a little.

"Here you are!" Mummy presents me with a whole sweet. Claire and Keith have to share bites of hers. It doesn't feel right somehow, competing now, against the family I share with all the time, when Mummy is at Christianburg. Then it dawns on me that my mother no longer knows how to play with us. Having lived apart for so long we've become her pupils, out

73

on the sportsfield, prompted to compete in the sprint event Sports Day fashion, for a prize from the P.E. teacher.

All the same, our August holidays were a wonderful chance for a chat.

"Why don't you live in Georgetown and take care of us yourself, Mummy?" I put it to her as we hurried to Lamaha Street for the bus.

"Because my headmaster won't give me de blasted transfer to another school!" Grey streaked her black hair these days and her middle finger sported a bunion from holding a writing pen so often. School teachers use pens a lot.

"Why not?" I wanted to understand but did not wish to cause her pain.

"He don't say why not. I asked and asked but he just won't do it. I suppose he don't like me because . . . I had money, until a little before just now. And I admit I was proud of meself. Now, as a low-paid teacher with three children to feed I still acting poor-great, but he got me at he mercy. More and more often I feel like leaving, but if I walk out of this job without getting a release from my Principal, I probably wouldn't ever be hired for another teaching job in this country. That's the stupid colonial rule in B.G." Mummy wasn't so much hurt as angry.

"But I'll show him and everyone else" she declared coolly and calmly, "I'll show them. I'll give my kids a first class education. No matter what they do to me!" Her face mysteriously lost the girlishness it seemed to have had. It aged and became womanly all of a sudden. Then Claire and I set about dealing Keith playful cuffs and gentle head slaps for making us proud of him. We'd learnt only hours before that he'd just won a scholarship to attend St Stanislaw's Catholic Boys College in Georgetown!

Mummy walked behind us on the road smiling as broadly as a giant water lily bloom.

"Mi riddle, mi-riddle, mi-ree. Me father had a tree.

74

"What's the best holiday place, Keithy Beaty?"

"New York?"

"No. You're cold!"

"London?"

"Ice Cold!"

"Trinidad Carnival?"

"Dead cold! I'll tell you. It's home. Christianburg!"

"Girl, you stupidee or what?" Keith died laughing at me. "Your brains ent teach you nothing!"

Paradise for me was away from Bishops and Olivia. Home! What a cruise to Christianburg! Up the Demerara past riverbend upon riverbend of uncut virgin forest, of giant mora, green-heart and silverbally trees which have stood since the dawn of time. That's what they told me the trees were, but I could make out only kapok and mango trees from a distance. Here and there I'd glimpse a village clearing of unpainted, wooden huts thatched with trulie palm fronds, Amerindian style.

Disturbed by the steamer's swells, powerful caymans, looking exactly like crocodiles to me, would launch into the water from along uninhabited river stretches. Out of gunshot reach, circling against the bright blue were carrion crows, hawks and swallowtails.

Just a few miles before Christianburg is that secret fearful place of our family's survival, before my mother's job paid so-so and Mudsie's bakery business made her well-to-do enough to employ a house servant. It's there, between the trees. No, . . . there . . . Or . . . no, . . . no . . . I can't find it without Granny Adrianna.

It was her secret 'sly-farm' on Crown land. Where we canoed to, silent and invisible as spirits in the pre-dawn, meringue-white mist; and rowed away from at sunsleep, our blackness blended into the night's; our dug-out craft laden to the gunwhales with farm vegetables and fruit. I haven't gone there since I was about ten. That secret farm meant survival for our poor black family for years. How else could our family avoid starvation? Protect itself from the ravages of malnutrition? Or from death when a weakened body was struck by a minor illness? I well remember Mary Nicholas who lived near Mudsie. Mary went to the Great Beyond one Easter, leaving three young motherless sons. Never having enough to eat, she sent to us constantly, requesting any vegetables we could help out with. She died in her twenties.

By 1959, one third of all our men in the colony were unemployed. People were sailing and flying to England to find work. Even my father left for London to 'rebuild the Mother Country' in 1946, when I was about three. The pity was he never looked back to help us properly. And our women? If you'd advertised a servant's job in Georgetown, you'd get over two hundred black hopefuls of all ages, willing to work like the proverbial. They'd fetch and carry six days a week, ten hours a day, with skimpy meals thrown in, for twenty-five dollars a month. Which of our mothers could raise a family on that? The government had no welfare benefits then. It paid only a pension of five dollars if you survived as long as Granny Adrianna to collect it. You had to look to your wits, your brawn and your family to survive.

Granny Adrianna persuaded herself that the Midas-rich family in Buckingham Palace would neither know nor care about the difference it made to their money-box, if she slashed and cleared a bit of South American jungle and grew bananas, cassavas, eddoes, yams and sweet potatoes secretly to eat. And since 'nothing's for nothing', old Granny Adrianna certainly paid for her farm. She gathered in produce which was often past its best because she stole visits to the farm haphazardly, only when her grandson, or a Church sister or I could farm with her. She paid by being constantly tense and ever alert to jaguars, boa-constrictors, venomous labaria snakes and caymans which would attack if she ever farmed alone or was careless.

Her body, never robust, paid a price in joint pains from having laboured in the broiling, equatorial sun one moment then in the pelting rain that followed. She ached from mosquito bites, malaria, ant bites, wasp stings, sand fly swarms, thorn pricks, mud parasites and chigoes in her toes. She ached when we, her great grand picknee, were also stung and bitten. Her heart pounded as we all paddled homewards, blanketed in the blackness. Precisely because we had to remain hidden for safety, water craft could collide with us, since their captain had no idea we were on the river.

I helped Granny Adrianna farm without understanding farming because the gaps in the picture were too large. We'd plant maize, sugarcane, bananas, pumpkins, tomatoes, then leave and never see them grow but hope the weeds didn't choke them, the insects didn't eat them or the sun didn't wither them. Months later we'd steal back to a grass choked clearing where some plants still struggled valiantly, others had died or had been flattened by a hurricane. Half an hour of wielding long sticks and cutlasses flushed snakes from the grass before we could even get near to the plants. Working backs to each other we'd face outwards constantly scanning for jaguars. Having lit the cooking fire quickly we weeded, propped up branches, tall-tied vines and harvested whatever the insects, birds and bats hadn't consumed. I never braved the mere fifty metres to the river alone to fetch water for the seedlings. I knew I'd be no match for the swift, powerful caymans lurking about which would drown me and turn the river brown-red feasting.

And was our food seasoned with joy? Our family shrouded the abundance on our table in secrecy or else "the Forest Ranger might hear tales and jail us for gardening for free on the Royal Family's land, out there behind God's back". We also knew well enough to share our produce with certain families who sent to ask us to help them out. Not Mary Nicholas' family but others. When our family was past hunger and baking had earned Mudsie enough wealth, she could no longer live with the fears of those sporadic garden visits, the danger of unable-to-swim Granny Adrianna capsizing and drowning. So on a faint-moon night, Mudsie cut the canoe's mooring rope loose from the cocoa tree at the water's edge and watched it sweep in a lonely, wanderer's dance down the silver-tinted Demerara River in the direction of Georgetown.

Here we are, moored at Mr Oxley's wharf at Christianburg, disembarking for our holiday at home. Remembering my last holiday I riddle to myself: "Mi-riddle, Mi-riddle, Mi-ree. Me father had a tree . . . What makes the least sense to me? You'll never guess. It's Mummy's mathematics!"

"Come up Wismar Hill with me. It's only three miles from Mudsie's. We building a Housing Scheme," Mummy invited me proudly.

"What's that?" We were walking away from Christianburg, up Wismar Road.

"Three hundred houses. Some to rent. Some for families to buy. The British Government sending in a bit of money. That should help make we lives better. Imagine! Putting up three hundred new houses. The British people afraid we would make the colony impossible to govern if all they keep sending in is troops." Mummy sometimes spoke in. riddles which I couldn't unravel.

"Not everybody could get into the Scheme. I got in even though I am a woman without a husband." Her pride was obvious.

"How that happen?" I was impressed.

"The local Guiana Government signed a paper saying that it will guarantee me the bank loan for the house because I been a government teacher for over ten years. And I intend to teach for this government 'till I retire or drop down dead." She was now puffing up the sand track.

"Well, getting into the Scheme was easy, nuh Mummy?" I spoke admiringly.

"Easy, me backside! Hard no hell, it was! I had to come up with a down-payment of five hundred dollars. Who got that sort of money around here to lend? So I had to join and 'throw a box'. Thank God I just paid my 'box-hand' to the bank last week."

Our African tradition had come to the rescue for raising large sums through the practice of 'throwing a box'. Ten persons, who knew and trusted each other, pledged to pool fifty dollars each person, every month, for ten months. They placed the money each month with the same trustworthy 'box-holder'. Then, each participant took turns to collect their 'box-hand', the sum of five hundred dollars; a different person collecting his or hers each month. Mummy drew the tenth box-hand and it ensured her downpayment on the house.

"Why you building . . ." she did not let me finish.

"Mother has, Father has . . . and blessed is the child that's got its own," Mummy warbled the lyrics of a Billie Holliday jazz song.

"Why you looking so puzzled chile? Who wouldn't want a house? I want to be me own big woman, turning me own key in me own lock! Right?"

"Is just that . . . how much you gun have to pay back each month?" I wavered between criticism and curiosity.

She told me, and knowing Mummy's salary I said, "Well, you got only ten dollars left after you pay on your house." How could I voice my fears? "Ten dollars can't feed you and look after you. So how you gun get the rest of the money to pay Olivia, and our Georgetown rent, and our light bill and our food and clothes and books . . ."

"God will provide!" Mummy snapped the lid down tightly on the subject.

I knew then that my mother had no head for mathematics.

Eleven

"Why she Mummy got to drop we off at the party? We ent babies. Then, she gun pick us up she self at midnight! Lawd, she embarrassing! She couldda let we walk over with Patsy Cambridge and the other girls," Claire mumbled fuming.

Holidays at Christianburg were an opportunity for partying. Allowed to dance at the 'Fete-fo-so' at Mackenzie School we ached for a chance to eye the boys. I said nothing but hoped to catch a glimpse of that adorable heartbreaker, Roger Hinds. Handsome, green-eyed, my age, his faint lisp made my heart pound. Possessing a complexion the colour of a lightly done pancake, he was considered a catch and while I felt I lacked the looks to attract him, I could still drool from afar. As things turned out I even had one heart thumpingly marvellous dance with him, but declined the offer to take a stroll outside. He was particularly busy for the rest of the evening making sure that he obliged all the girls who were eager to dance with him.

Re-acquainting ourselves with the Christianburg community and showing off our clothes to no one in particular, we went to the market each shopping morning of the August holidays.

"'Morning Miss Irene. 'Morning Miss Marjorie," we greeted the 'rat women', prostitutes from the 'Bad House' near Mudsie's home. Drilled in being polite to everyone, since they bought our bread, we never snubbed these despised women. Mudsie had said that in moments of personal danger rat women could be relied on to help you, when more respectable people might refuse to help for fear of being beaten up.

"'Morning Sergeant Chalmers," to the local plod in black serge.

"Miz Antoine, good Mornin!" Mudsie's French West Indian customer and a small-business woman herself. She spoke French patois.

"Eh, Miz Nelson Grandpicknee, Lawd how y'all growin. Keep good."

"Sister Bonnet, Sister Barker. Granny said to tell you 'Howdy'," we called out the standard lie to members of Granny Adrianna's Brethren church.

Strolling from one end of Christianburg to the other in newly sewn, adult styled skirts and blouses, we were attempting to be feminine without being girlish. Going out clothes now had no sashes at the waist. We heard no ". . . put on your socks and tie a hair ribbon on your plaits before you walk de road!" We also puffed up Wismar Hill to visit Mummy's bungalow-in-the-building.

Across the way from those two bedroom concrete block and iron roof buildings, stood a new wooden house, unpainted but well built in a fenced compound on village land.

"Come and meet someone. Calls himself a 'Man of God'." Mummy guided me over the sand trail to the compound. I had become used to Mummy's proud introductions of me to this person and that, "Meet Mona, me Bishops daughter." Then I was expected to behave with restraint and to speak Bishops Properly.

He was expecting us. A slim, thirty-ish, dark man of African descent whose grin revealed a wealth of gold capped teeth. His head was completely shaved which was startling to my eyes, unique and strange in our village and calculated to make him the instant focus of attention. He led us briskly into his office which had a desk, a chair and a few religious books.

"Meet Shalto," Mummy said as we sat down. He took up a pen.

81

"You are at Bishops," he said as if interviewing me, but looking down and scribbling instead on his writing pad. "And what of your stewardship at that school?" he spoke in a squeezed voice. What on earth did he mean?

I was not impressed with what seemed like a show of terrible manners and bad playacting. In my dealings with certain whites it was not unusual for them to concentrate on other things while speaking to me, to invite me to feel insignificant. So, here was this man appearing to write furiously while asking me questions. Yet I noticed that he could not quite pull it off. He scribbled only random words, not full sentences. I chose to be mute.

"Does the child not understand me?" his tone was superior.

"How have you carried out your duties at Bishops?" Mummy rephrased the question quietly, calmly, helpfully.

"What duties?" I asked them both, wondering what business it was of his.

"All of your duties?" Shalto said grandly, still pushing the pen with jerks and flourishes. I decided to remain silent. What right did he have to my confidence, I wanted to know! Mummy had on her 'trying to please' face, and was urging me with silent desperation to co-operate.

"Oh, the Bishops girl has carried out all her duties well?" he spoke mockingly. "She has done everything perfectly!"

I scented menace and retreated to that first refuge of wise men and natives . . . stony silence.

When he glanced up and caught my cold, distant eyes he announced, "Oh, you're proud, are you? You think you are greater than us here? Well, let me tell you this, I have the power to turn the secrets that are hidden beneath your skirts and to expose them to the world! I know your hidden doings and your dark thoughts and I urge you to be humble about your wickedness and turn to good. I advise you to confess what you have been up to at school."

His speech flowed smoothly to my debater's ear. He seemed

used to saying this bosh and getting results. I looked at bits of food between his unbrushed gold teeth and disliked him intensely.

I wondered why he was attacking me, of whom I presumed he knew nothing. Worse, why was my mother putting up with this undeserved verbal slapping of me? He seemed to be angling for a verbal fight in order to gain the upper hand, so I decided not to engage in battle at all. I became as silent as Kunia Persaud.

"Be not stiff-necked. Accept rebuke with love!" His fingernails were dirty, his face badly shaven, his shirt grubby. Spit now flew as he worked himself up but as I sat erect, wore a tight-lipped superior smile, a glazed look in my eyes and never spoke, he stopped eventually and angrily told us to leave. Walking out of the compound I controlled my fury to ask, "Who is he really? Not this 'Man of God' stupidness, but who?" Mummy was unruffled, as if nothing in the world had happened.

"He is Olivia's common-law husband. He heads a religious community that I'm part of. We joined . . . Mudsie too . . . recently. We've built him this House of Worship . . . he advises us on . . . things." I remained mute long enough for the silence to congeal, as we walked down the hill.

"Was it his idea to have Olivia take care of us?" I watched my temper and observed Mummy.

"Yes. Or I wouldn'ta had anyone to do it." Mummy's voice was tinged with gratitude.

Now how was I going to tell her that we were always hungry in Olivia's care, that our valuables were disappearing, our clothes were becoming shabby because she spent nothing on repairs, that I was embarrassed it took two months to pay a fifty cent Home Ec fee because I now got no pocket money. Would Mummy listen this time any better than she had when I'd complained of Mr McGowan? Even if she listened could we find another guardian? Someone kinder than we'd had? Would my voice outweigh the voice of this advisor-man, in my mother's ear? Not from what I had just seen. The nightmare of cruelty had thrown its fog once again over me and I felt unable to help my mother to see this.

"Did this Shalto advise you to build a house? That bungalow?" I was hoping . . .

"Yes, or a golden opportunity I wouldda been blind to. I wouldda felt I couldn't afford it." My heart stopped beating. Between my mother and me clearly lay a gulf, a ravine; as distinct in its outline as an alpine river valley.

I detested this man whose advice my mother valued. I knew I could never embrace his religious court which my mother had just joined. And it occurred to me that if my mother's house was built a stone's throw from his House of Worship he might often visit. Should that happen, Mummy's residence would never become my home. Home would remain Mudsie's bakery. My mother and I had grown miles apart. My heart stopped when I realised that. I felt as cold as death, striding with sand in my leather shoes, the midday glare threatening to give me a headache, the sun parching my hair on that scorching day. Here, dramatically, was my answer to a riddle Keith had once dangled before my mind: "Mi riddle, Mi riddle, Me ree. Me father had a tree. When do you feel like ice in the middle of a bread oven?"

Twelve

"His name is Elvis Presley," said two blond Bishops classmates newly arrived with their American Embassy parents from Albuquerque, New Mexico. This was September of my third year at Bishops.

"Doesn't he look like a Greek god!" They passed the almost-holy record album cover around. Then they performed a sort of adoration our Lower Fourth classmates had never witnessed. In rich American accents they cried, "Ooooh! Oh my god!"

They clutched their chests, mock-screamed, pulled at handfuls of hair, became breathless, pretended to go weak at the knees and made bubbly, throaty gurgles. Classmates kissed Elvis' picture on the album cover and goggled at the Americans' routine.

"He's more handsome than the Everly Brothers!" these hip girls declared and the rest of us agreed.

"He sings 'Blue Suede Shoes' and 'Heartbreak Hotel'. Oooh!" the Americans said, and then repeated the routine. American teenagers were all doing this when they saw their teen-idols, we were told. We were fascinated by this new idea of the teenager, because in our society you were a child until you married or got a fulltime job. Then you were treated as an adult, and there was nothing in-between. This was both a new word and a new idea, 'the teenager'.

In a month our white classmates had learned to mimic the routine perfectly and the pantomime began when someone said,

'Oh Elvis! Isn't he handsome! I dig him the most! I wanna diiiiieee!"

Wonderful though he seemed, I could not respond to Elvis for half a second. Although, according to the world atlas, we were a South American country, culturally we were West Indians. Our men toured with the West Indies cricket team, we spoke neither Portuguese nor Spanish but English; we drank tea rather than coffee from our neighbour Brazil and musically we played steel bands and sang calypsoes. For most of us who were of African descent the adored singer was a calypsonian from the West Indian island of Grenada, The Mighty Sparrow. His songs boasted that dozens of women were wild about him: Rose, Maria, Jean and Dinah, Rosita and Clementina. He sang about science and politics; about Sputnik being shot into space orbit with a solitary tragic passenger, the Russian dog Laika, doomed to die and hurtle in space for aeons.

> Oh yes, they trying they best but they making a mess
> O de Russian satellite!
> They should be all sent to prison
> For de dog that they poison
> In de Russian satellite.
> Two Sputniks in de sky have everybody hypnotised
> But Sparrow is very sorry for de poor little puppy
> In de Russian Satellite.

His other popular song of that moment told of the Americans leaving Trinidad, our neighbour in the Caribbean, after the oil-fields had been pumped dry.

"De Yankees gone, West Indians take over now!" he boasted.

Above all, we loved the fact that his calypsoes, sung in West Indian dialect, were usually naughty songs with double meanings. These we boldly chorused in front of the teachers from England and they hadn't a clue.

When, in the holidays, I sang Sparrow to Mudsie who had

no radio to hear him, she'd double over. "You Mona! Ha! Ha! You'se a caution! Ha!Ha! Oh lawd child, don't kill me! Ha! Ohh! This laughing hurting me belly! Ha! Ha! What a wotliss man dat Sparrow is! Ha! Ha!" We'd dance a while to my singing until a customer came into the shop to buy.

It was as different "as midnight-moonlight is from midday-sunlight" to be seated every school morning on the floor in the assembly hall at Bishops listening to selected overtures and excerpts from 'A Midsummer's Night Dream', 'The Magic Flute', 'Carmen' or 'La Bohème'. Miss Bacchus gave us a brief summary of the music beforehand to help us understand it. Sometimes we listened to arias sung in Italian, German or French by Maria Callas, Elizabeth Schwarzkopf or Renata Tebaldi. On rare occasions I felt acknowledged when the 'American Negroes' Marian Anderson and Paul Robeson sang. My ears were more attuned, however, to the familiar religious choral works which were played in the department stores at Christmas time, including 'The Hallelujah Chorus' from 'The Messiah' and 'Jesu Joy of Man's Desiring'.

The school rose quietly when the Headmistress entered and strode on to the stage. The quiet was followed by full-throated renditions of elegant Anglican hymns, with half of the school singing the descant. Within my first year I had memorised the verses of most of the hymns we sang regularly, like 'O Worship the King', 'Praise, my soul, the King of Heaven' or 'Hills of the North, Rejoice!'.

Then 'Molly the Mop' Harris, our secret name for the Headmistress, led us in Anglican prayers. After all, we were constantly reminded that although Bishops was now a Government school, funded by my grandmother's rates and taxes, there was still a tradition to maintain. Bishops High School for Girls had been founded by English clergy for the daughters of those English church members who had come out to the colony

87

for a few years. Looking at the present pupils though, an increasing number in the lower school was dark skinned, most likely recent scholarship winners. I recognised by their names that Hindu and Muslim pupils of East Indian descent were also dotted about in good measure. They too sang the hymns but with little enthusiasm.

The service of hymns and prayers over, we listened to the school notices and the names of girls on detention (Disgrace! Disgrace!), before filing back to class and lessons. I'd kept my nose reasonably clean. Here, my word, were girls who had earned three order marks, were therefore given a conduct detention, and were now on to their second or third detention!

It was falling in love with calypsoes that 'dropped me backside on the thorns o' the plimpla bush' as they say.

"Miss Bacchus, can't we sing our own songs? Cy Grant sings them on the B.B.C. Even Harry Belafonte sings them in New York." I was bold enough to plead one day in singing.

"Which songs?" she asked.

"He sings 'Mama look a boo-boo' and . . ."

"Look, we have to learn an anthem for Commemoration Day Service at St George's Cathedral. It's 'Exultate Jubilate'. And all the music for the Christmas cantata; we've learnt only 'When Gabriel came to Mary' but there are another twelve melodies to master. Please don't waste my time." With a sweep of her articulate arms we began with the vowel "OOO", to warm up our voices. I felt small, dismissed, unable to marshal the right words to explain nicely that all of the melodies we were learning were white music. However much I enjoyed other people's music I wished to sing my own as well. Especially in this place where music was treated with respect. Weren't any of our 'clean' calypsoes worthy of school respect? Any of our folk songs? Must we sing of Guiana only when the tone poem echoes English music?

Not long afterwards I looked at the lovely meals we cooked

in Home Ec. Baked stuffed potatoes, roast beef and Yorkshire pudding, carrot salad, chocolate eclairs and trifles. All mouth-wateringly perfect, all Bishops food, most of which I could never cook at home in our rice-growing country. Those imported potatoes, carrots, tins of cream and cocoa were too expensive for our ordinary budget, even for Mudsie's budget. And a roast! After long talks with my chubby, brown skinned cooking partner Barbara Niles I said, "Barbara, you ask. Just say, 'Miss Welcome, can't we cook our own people's food, metagee or foo-foo or pepperpot?' She'll listen to you."

"You want me to get wrong-up? I ent asking nothing."

"But you could explain that your family's going to live in Kumasi because your father will teach at the University there. So you need to learn to cook African food." Barbara's family was off to newly independent Ghana which had been the British colony called the Gold Coast. We were impressed by this.

"You is the big mouth, you ask yourself!" play-it-safe Barbara said. We laughed quietly at our fear of even asking.

So, in English, "But can't we study a West Indian novel, please Miss?"

"Mona, the Caribbean is yet to produce writing worthy of the name of literature, but when such works have been produced, rest assured we will be glad to teach them. Whom did you have in mind?" This Mistress with an M.A. from an English University was English born and bred. She was particularly thin but attractive, grey eyed, with black shoulder length hair, intelligent and usually approachable.

"I don't know anybody Miss," I confessed, "but is just that on Mrs Thorne's radio there's a BBC Programme called 'London Calling the Caribbean'. The announcer is supposed to be a writer too."

"Who?"

"Andrew Salkey is his name, I think, Miss."

"Mona you're off on a tangent again . . ."

"Miss, he interviewed George Lamming, and Samuel Selvon, and C. L. R. James and Derek Walcott."

"We're studying Shakespeare now Mona. I trust you've heard of him."

"But after this Miss, can't we read something? A Guianese novel? I've heard of Edgar Mittelholzer."

"Well then, read his work yourself Mona, you're holding up the entire class. Now, who was reading the part of Titania yesterday?"

The class giggled with relief that they had had an answer to our question, which many had discussed in break-time and had wished to raise, without having to feel put down themselves. I felt hurt beyond words. We read together *A Midsummer Night's Dream* in that rich language we found so baffling and foreign while a rage germinated within me. Besides, were there no West Indian plays worthy of study for later on?

Slowly I felt invaded by a feeling to which I could not put a name. A feeling which festered from hearing day in day out, week in week out, years on end that British Guiana is "a backward country, with an under-developed economy". I was aware of this awful feeling every time our country dances were called primitive dance and were laughed at but not taught at Bishops. Similar European dances were called folk dances; these we learnt and performed for displays. The feeling surfaced when our Art was called Primitive Art unless our ideas had influenced Picasso for his 'Head of a bull', made with a bicycle saddle and handle-bar. Only then was our work considered proper Fine Art. Our art room had many works by Turner, Reynolds, Gainsborough, Henry Moore, Leonardo da Vinci and Constable, but nothing by our local carvers or painters. Equally, there was no African art. No Black American art. How did I feel? As invisible as our absent artists.

The culture of the school made me feel ashamed and stupid to ask for our own music, our food, our novels, poetry and plays, our art or our dances although I knew I should never feel this way.

Ghana's becoming independent of Britain earlier in the year, 1957, the first Black African nation to do so, changed the thinking of our black population forever. We felt proud to see Africans dressed in their colourful costumes. Many had been educated in Britain and were equally comfortable in Saville Row suits. Pictures showed them weighed down with gold adornments, wearing golden ceremonial sandals, borne shoulder high, some of them on carved stools. They were celebrating with drumming, setting out to rule themselves. We openly laughed at the British Government's line that 'black people cannot govern themselves'. This year we had come to regard what Ghana had achieved as our right too, not any longer a privilege to be earned. We listened to senior pupils saying quietly in school, "We want to govern ourselves".

While I adored History, I had no clear idea of when or why the different nationalities came to B.G. nor of the history of my African descended people in the land. I was told, "B.G. is too young to have a history to speak of."

"But Miss, my great grandmother told me about Quamina Gladstone and his son Jackie. They led a slave rebellion at Vreed-en-Hoop."

"What rebellion are you on about now Mona?"

"The one on the estate owned by the British Prime Minister Gladstone."

"Which year was this, Mona?"

"I don't know Miss."

"Well then, why don't you first get your facts straight. We can't discuss it reasonably otherwise."

"But I do have my facts Miss. After the rebellion they jailed the White Minister on the estate for teaching the slaves to read the Bible. And he died in jail. And they named Smith's Congregational Church on Brickdam after that White Minister."

91

"Oh. You mean John Smith. Guiana's only martyr."

"Yes, that rebellion Miss. But please Miss, aren't all those other black people who died martyrs as well, Miss?"

"Mona, we aren't having a debate about it. You'll have to 'beat your own drum and dance all by yourself' as your people say. We can't keep going off at all angles! We have a topic to cover. Furthermore we're studying British History for the O level exams later. No other sort. Are we clear? So, we're on Page 39. Who'll read?"

In the orderly lesson which followed we wrote notes and looked attentive. I steeled myself not to cry. Barbara winked, wrote and passed me her note which read, 'VREED-EN-HOOP 1823.'

How could I feel proud of myself and my people if I knew little or nothing of our heroes, our heroines, our achievements? Since 'ours' were not taught, I believed 'ours' either did not exist or 'ours' were inferior to 'theirs' of the British and white people. A fight had broken out within me; to learn Bishops knowledge while rejecting the Bishops messages that whatever was local or black was to be ignored or spoken of in words which invited us to despise it. It was unbearable to feel 'less than' or 'not good enough'.

"No, Mona. You simply cannot pull out of the debate at this eleventh hour!" the mistress in charge of the debating team was speaking sternly. I liked and modelled myself on her and tried to please her. She was local, dark skinned and held a degree from St Andrews University, in Scotland.

"But Miss, I could tell someone else the points and they could debate it. I just have so much homework to do," I reasoned.

"Well, so would every other girl. You can't let the school down like this, and certainly not against St Stanislaw's College! You really have no choice." She was firm.

We debated, we won and I walked home alone, sobbing, broken, feeling filthy. Neither Mudsie nor Granny Adrianna was at home in Georgetown to bandage me up.

In arguing for the proposition that 'Chastity before marriage is the ideal' I had been forced to look at my family and our black community. Not everyone had had children after marriage, a vast number of men and women had become parents before. Even my father had had an 'outside son' with someone else before he'd married Mummy. While my African Slave descended society did not strongly condemn this, for reasons bound up in hundreds of years of slave history, the points I was forced to speak in the debate certainly did. Those points were some other society's values, and speaking them produced in me a painful sense of complete disloyalty to my people. Even my own Granny Adrianna had had Mudsie and Uncle Benjamin while a widow, then three more children in her later, second marriage. How could I explain, and to whom, the feeling of being crushed between two worlds?

Next day, amid congratulations from Victoria House members for trouncing Saints, "Now what's this all about? You aren't withdrawing?"

"Please Miss, is just that I have so much homework," I lied.

"But you're so good at debating, you simply must . . ."

"I can't Miss, homework," I mumbled, baffled to have come to an unimaginable place where I was being hurt by, and had to run away from, Bishops approved 'success'.

How could I admit, explain, when I did not fully understand it myself, that school heaven was destroying me? My people and I were presented to girls of other races in the school, so they too believed it, as being backward and under-developed, with nothing worth teaching to others and nothing worth learning about. We were spoken of as primitive, immoral, without accomplishments or heroes, with only a slave history to talk about if one could be bothered to talk about it. On the other hand we were taught to regard as admirable, people who had bought, captured, shipped, sold, worked, ill-treated, ill-fed, branded, whipped, raped, sometimes beaten to death or by other means killed millions of my people. Bishops looked up to those who had made fortunes and become leaders in British society from having had slaves. Like Prime Minister Gladstone. We were being invited to copy the ideals they spoke about but didn't live.

That conflict was ever with us. Right here in Bishops was the brown skinned descendant of one of Britain's wealthiest aristocratic whisky families. We were proud of this mistress for having been an Oxford scholar who had gained first class honours. Her Guianese line was descended from her nineteenth century British aristocratic forefather who had never bothered to marry her Guianese slave foremother.

A cornerstone of slavery in British Guiana had been the non-existence of real slave families for centuries. As slaves had no rights to wives or husbands, slave marriages had no legal standing. Slaves were bred as cattle were, mated with whomever the master decided, at times with the master himself. They could be sold, and were at any time taken from each other and from that plantation forever. The children of slaves belonged to the master and were also sold at his will, from about two years old. Slave parents had no power to protect their children, their partner or even themselves from floggings, from being worked to death, from rape or from sale. And at any rate adult slaves in our region lived nine years at the most, if they were extremely lucky, from the time of capture to the time of death, so hard was their lot, working fourteen hours a day and so wretched was their treatment. Yet our people developed a family system to make sure that we'd survive. And survived we had, after slavery was abolished. Why were we now being treated to opinions which invited us to feel self contempt rather than pride?

Loving English literature was a struggle. I embraced then held it at a tremendous distance from my head and heart. Otherwise I would have been destroyed by its picture of my people as both ugly and evil. How could I love being black? The bad feelings had surfaced everytime I dealt with the words Black Friday, blackmail, black humour, black list, black ball, 'that has surely blackened her name', black mouth, Black Maria, blackguard, black looks, the Black Hole of Calcutta, 'he's walking around in a black fog', black as sin, practising the black arts, black heart, black flag, black thoughts, a black mark against you, black cloud, 'you're in the teacher's black books', 'the censor blacked out those lines in the newspaper', and the black Prince of Darkness—the Devil. In this school my colour had only negative ideas presented with it, like black witches, black magic, grime, dirt, disease, the black dog of despair, the figure of death, and on and on. Oh Lawd! Who could be proud of herself in such a school?

At the very same time we were bombarded with white images as altogether admirable. The White House, white witches, the white flag, the white wedding dress, pure and white, the white rose of the House of York, the white knight, clean and white, white bread, white linen, the Great White Queen of England, Victoria; a white lie, White Hall, whitewash the house, Whitsunday, white Christmas. Who in Bishops would choose to be black in a world so seemingly one-sided? Worse, I doubted that other girls, taught these exact opinions mixed in with valuable knowledge, would ever in their hearts at the end of the years at Bishops, respect or like black people. I knew of older Bishops girls who clearly by the things they said despised themselves for being black. Classmates did not usually see what I was objecting to. When they sometimes did, they kept quiet for fear of getting into trouble.

Would Mudsie listen to me? Would Granny Adrianna believe or even understand what I was saying? Would Claire agree with me against the almighty Bishops? Which staff member would? And I knew better than to try to tell Mummy, bedazzled as she was by what she imagined Bishops to be. I took to arguing in class, thumped by the sheer volume of destructive ideas, school day after school day.

Coming to Bishops in the morning filled me with dread. No

surprise then, that my second conduct detention was given for 'chronic lateness to school without a reasonable excuse'. By the end of the school year I'd lost count of detentions; for pelting a cricket ball up the mango tree as I'd done all my primary school life, for shouting in the corridors during break time, for sliding down the bannisters, and for slinging my *Songs of Praise* hymn book through the class window into the mango tree after singing a hymn in assembly about the heathens in their blindness bowing down to wood and stone. I put a thumb tack, pointed end upwards, in the teacher's chair, on to which Miss Quok lowered herself. During another lesson the class giggled non-stop for half a period until Mrs D'Orban discovered that my shirt and tie were being worn back to front, and that my shoes, which had a distinctive inward curve, had been put on left to right and now pointed to the opposite walls of the classroom. I was invited to step outside.

"I hear dem people calling you name," warned head servant Dora. "You'd better look sharp!" she advised, giving nothing else away.

All went calmly for weeks. Then, while dressing together after Scottish dancing in the hall, we did that for an hour in PE, a newly arrived Scottish girl was told by me that she and her father's regiment, the Argyll and Sutherland Highlanders, should all blessed well go back to where they'd blessed well come from, because Guianese could not blessed well go to Scotland. We wouldn't be let in. Even if we were, we couldn't tell the Scots what to blessed well do. So who were the troops to blessed well storm into my country to 'keep the peace'? And anyway, who told her that she was good enough for Bishops without blessed well sitting scholarship? The distressed girl was escorted by a bevy of classmates to the staff room door. It hadn't crossed my mind that Mrs Russell, our Victoria House leader, a tough, chain smoking, straight talking Latin mistress was also a Scot!

She bowled me what looked like a bumper at the Christmas break-up. Victoria House members, all one hundred and something of them, were told, ". . . and Victoria House has come last this term in the school's competition for the Conduct Shield. Thanks to one individual. One girl who has utterly disgraced this entire House. Never before has this happened, that one pupil alone has earned more order marks than all the senior pupils put together! I hope you'll let her know of your extreme displeasure. That disgrace to the proud tradition of Victoria House is Mona Williams!"

About one hundred steely-cold eyes stared, carved me up and cut me dead as House members filed out of the geography room without a single word in my direction. Further humiliation was waiting in the assembly hall where we would gather for the final ceremony and the presentation of trophies before break-up. Yet, 'Even the devil has a friend!', as the saying goes. One unforgettable senior, Jeanette Alphonso alone, broke rank, came over and hugged me around the shoulders.

"Never mind. Never mind. Don't cry . . ." her thin brown face was kindly, her soft voice comforting. How I wished that my own mother could react like that even if she could not understand.

The Board of Governors considered and voted against my expulsion in view of the past honours I had brought to Bishops, and recommended that I be given one term's grace to mend my ways.

"From what dey saying in de staff room, you head is in de tiger's mouth!" Dora confided darkly. "You better soft-soap de position next term."

"Mona's misbehaviour has become chronic," said the school report without outlining exactly what I had done, so I confessed to no-one anything of my plight. Certainly not with Olivia in our midst. Mummy was not sure what those English Mistress' terribly educated phrases meant by, 'her conduct leaves much to be desired', but Mudsie's eyes were haunted with understanding.

Seeing that my time at Bishops was beginning to resemble the smashed, precious tea pot of my mother's golden dreams, I wished for two Christmas gifts. Firstly, someone to talk to, who would not tell me how privileged I was to be at Bishops and that, "You should put your head down and bat steadily and stop all this stupidness!"

Secondly, should my mother find out that I was within a hair's breadth of expulsion she'd flog me, so I wanted to know the quickest and most effective way to end my life.

Thirteen

"Lord, even if you won't come, can't you send?" I cajoled, remembering Nora's arrival. What a welcome wonder it turned out to be that Mummy, holidaying with us, allowed us out at night on our own in big Georgetown.

Claire and I, by now fifteen and fourteen, spent all of Saturday straightening and styling our hair with metal combs and curling irons heated on the kerosene stove. Hours were lavished on ironing our school blouses and wide floral dress skirts to perfection. Then we polished our flat going-out shoes which no one would see anyway, bathing and perfuming ourselves, lacquering our fingernails, powdering and finally applying claret-coloured lipstick. We walked nearly three kilometres with about four hundred other Christmas holiday revellers to the assembly point on Brickdam, opposite the Alms House. Our chosen band, the Debonaires, was one of five playing through the streets that night. The steel band tuned up, its sixteen good-looking black young men displayed crisp, open necked shirts and pressed pants. One looked at me and I wanted to diiiiie! They beat out snatches of calypsoes on tuned oil drums which were mounted on wheeled frames for pushing through the streets. A few of the steel band players who were eyeing the crowd knew they looked deliciously handsome! Girls pretended not to look at them but broke up giggling. Then the band burst forth with a wild popular calypso.

At this, around 7 p.m., we danced off energetically in long

lines stretched across the street, arms around the waists of the strangers we found ourselves next to. We line-danced, feet jumping in small, springing, joyful steps, voices loudly singing naughty Sparrow lyrics. This was tramping to the pulsating rhythm of West Indian steel band music along streets cleared of all traffic by the police. The crowd, growing to thousands after an hour, meandered up this street and down that one, drenched in sweat. Claire and I chatted briefly and exchanged names with the boys on either side of us, then called, "Hi Whaple! Ullrich, Wainey! Roger!" to our friends from Christianburg way. There weren't any Bishops girls about. Didn't you know? Bishops girls didn't tramp!

We disengaged ourselves from these boys to join on to the line of those boss-looking bannahs who were swaying wickedly and laughing heartily in front of us. Dropping out, ducking, diving and joining the other line-dancers, our eyes enjoyed a marvellous spectacle. As far as we looked there was a rippling ocean of arching bodies, wave upon wave undulating in rhythm, zig-zagging across the street, linking and surging, energetic and joyful, smiling, singing, shouting, sweating, hip swivelling, for miles and for hours. With arms linked around each others' waists in the line, the boy sometimes tried out sliding a hand too far up our sides but I gave their wandering fingers a particularly hard elbow jab to show I meant business. Prettier, preferred, rounder, gentler Claire achieved the same effect with swift cold stares. We felt thirsty but never tired, and who cared what time it was?

Panting into Bourda Market Square at midnight, lines formed into dance display circles, everyone took turns in the middle showing off, 'winding' naughtily and learning the latest moves, the Neck and Back and the Rengue. We enjoyed egging on those wickedly handsome high school boys who were also superb dancers. Much too soon the steel band's voice was stilled, and having exchanged names and addresses with the classy looking,

100

expensively dressed bannahs, Claire and I implied that we would be tramping behind another band, from a different starting point tomorrow night. As if Mummy would allow us! Though we enjoyed meeting them we never formed friendships with any of those boys whose families we did not know.

Yakking excitedly we cloud-stepped towards home, surrounded by other revellers, feeling like girlish women, attractive and utterly safe in a big city so early in the morning. Our bodies responded to our traditions of African music and community dance as drought-striken fields would have to gentle, warm, tropical rains.

Home at Christianburg Mummy informed me, "Got you a job over the river at Mckenzie for Christmas holidays. In Sandbach Parker . . . sales girl. You want the work?"

"You gun ask? Of course! How much they paying?"

"Mrs Liefmans says twelve dollars a week."

"Only? . . . better a little something than pure nothing nuh Mummy?" my tone was eager.

"To a starving picknee one milk-breast is better than a flat chest," she agreed.

Meeting the public, earning money, dressing in a tight working skirt, feeling a little grown up, all caused a smile as bright as if I'd had sixty-four teeth.

"Mummy, is all right with you if I try to get part-time work in the holidays in Georgetown. Make a lil money?"

"Which holidays you mean?" she was hesitant.

"School ones, May, August, Christmas." I meant religious ones too but didn't dare say that.

"You need the coppers nuh chile?" was Mummy's version of yes. The satisfying heart-hammers I felt were not about the money but about my ability to avoid coming home often.

The manner was off hand, the voice too casual when Mummy said out of the blue a week later, "You-all father write. He in

101

England. He want you-all to write he. Here. The address. Look this stamp. Put you-all letters in together."

Sitting as if shell-shocked I wondered if my head were really exploding. My supreme wish! Did old Granny Adrianna have a hand in this matter? Does Heaven sneak up on one like this? No thunder? No lightening? No tempest, flood, earthquake or volcano's upsurge to announce the arrival? Just wrapped in an ordinary sentence, "You-all father write . . .".

Outwardly speechless, my head was thundering with shouted orders. *Don't appear too eager. Your mother will feel jealous. Put off writing for a week so you'll think before you speak. Keep what you'll discuss to yourself or you'll create bad feelings with your mother. Better not write about other family members. That way no one can accuse you of 'showing the family stewpot to outsiders'. Will you ask him what he's done since he left the family? Might he say that it's none of your business? Will he really want to know you? Will he like you? What'll you call him? Edmund, Dad, Pop, Old man? What do you call a parent you haven't spoken to for most of your life? Will you ask for a photo seeing that you can't picture him after twelve years apart?*

Mummy always became absolutely deaf and mute at the sound of his name, which explains why my father was largely unknown to me.

Will you like him? Will he be understanding, kind? What on earth will you talk about, school? Not blessed likely seeing that you're up for expulsion. Ask him why he left and never gave money to support the family in all these years? Will you ask him for a bit of money for somethings? Wait a minute, was this heaven?

My longed-for heaven was proving difficult for this earthling.

Having a father I could speak to by letter rather than having the mere idea of a father alive somewhere in Britain, made my life happier. Ever so casually I was going to tell others at Bishops, like Joy Best and Cicely Rodway, "Well, my dad in England wrote me to say . . .". A father! What hope!

102

Yet hopeful of what, I had no idea. Perhaps my parents just might become a family again, seeing that although they had been separated they had not divorced in all these years.

Living with Olivia meant growing noticeably thinner, being pre-occupied with food, feeling tired and irritable, and developing cavities. Still school life glistened with starburst moments, despite expulsion hanging over me like a sword of Damocles. Handsome Mike Agostini, Trinidad's olympic sprinter, visited our assembly and set the hearts of the staff and pupils a-quiver. Then sixth former Carol Chan-Choon, with no experience at all, had the daring just the same to direct and enter a Russian play for the Secondary Schools' National Drama Festival. Incredibly, I was chosen for the leading role of Matryona over the other hopeful, my idol Sandra Williams. Although the play was unplaced in the finals it rebuilt my belief in myself. I decided to live as daringly as Carol Chan-Choon had done. Studying lesson topics carefully, arguing aloud no more, I was careful to write like a debater exactly what I had thought of poems and history topics. Teachers avoided making comments on my opinions but pointed out spelling mistakes and marked me fairly. By term's end, thank heavens, my marks had positioned me in the top half of the class in all my subjects. With that, the threat of expulsion was removed although I had earned one or two conduct detentions. Even then a restlessness was driving me to look beyond Bishops. But for what?

'What don't kill, will fatten', you could say of what happened because of my insatiable curiosity. You see, my eyes had refused to believe posters I gawped at in Bookers department store. A pale skinned ballerina in a stiff white tutu, was standing tall on the tip of one foot with the other leg shooting against the back of her head towards the sky. Incredible! The splits standing up. This was fair complexioned Helen Taitt, daughter of a prominent, extremely wealthy Georgetown doctor of African descent. Helen had recently returned to B.G. after years in New York and her recital at Queen's College featured selections from classical ballets in which she was partnered by George Chaffe, who had also trained in New York.

Lacking money to see her concert I nevertheless had the nerve to audition at her studio when a newspaper announced her setting up a School of Ballet. Ballet schools world-wide in those days did not usually accept black skinned dancers; Chinese pupils, yes, fair skinned 'others', perhaps, but a black dying swan? Don't be ridiculous! Defying the odds I was accepted by Miss Taitt and wondered how I would pay for lessons, food, pink tights, ribbons, ballet slippers, food, a black singlet which would be cut and sewn into a leotard, a kit bag and food.

Dressed in my best and bravest I pounded the pavement, a determined fourteen year old, asking for a part time job at every department store in Georgetown's commercial district, Water Street. The largest firm, Bookers, (long before it offered the world a prize for literature from its profits in B.G.) offered me much needed help: the promise of holiday jobs later and half-day work now, every Saturday in the children's shoe department. My sales girl position was unique also, same reason. Portuguese, Chinese and pale others as sales staff, yes; but a jet black sales girl? Come, come! However, I'd explained in Properly to the personnel manager, a former Bishops girl, "I attend Bishops . . ."

Breathlessly, I pelted to my first lesson at the School of Guiana Ballet in Dr Taitt's mansion, its huge formal living room tastefully converted into a European dance studio. From the moment I stood in that world that I had seen only in books devoted to the Royal Ballet — a world of barres, wooden floors, mirrors, spacious elegance, turned columns, ivory painted rooms and ballerinas' pictures on the walls; of directions softly spoken in French, of neat grooming, graceful lines of the arms, live piano music from Chopin's waltzes; of rozin, hard work, perspiration and discipline with smiles—I knew I had found the partner of my soul, dance. The gooseflesh and heart hammers confirmed that I had entered my own dream. My own school heaven. I knew immediately that dance would transform my life.

"Oooh!" I said like the girls who diiieeed for Elvis, "He hasn't come . . . but my word! He's definitely sent!"

Fourteen

During midterm break I explored the public areas of Dr Taitt's mansion and grounds. A massive sopadilla tree dominated the garden, and his dining suite was almost the size of our entire flat, with chairs designed straight out of Windsor Castle pictures. The School of Guiana Ballet was quiet and peaceful without pupils. I caught snatches of, "I dig that . . . yeah . . . cool man!" and recognised the voice of Miss Taitt's fiancé speaking on the office phone. Tall, boney and bearded, Mr Mason was a white beatnik from New York. He loved jazz, cigarettes, sophisticated jokes and discussing 'breaking free of the colonial mentality'.

Then, notes danced like crystal in the air; distinct, light, angular, sparkling, sharp. "I thought it was the radio. Was it you? Can you . . ."

"Play the piano?" she finished the sentence while I continued to admire the melody Miss Taitt fingered on the upright piano in the dance studio. "Yes, I went up to grade eight. I'm writing a musical," she said primly.

"Oh!" was all I could manage, my mouth dropping open.

"Part of, ummm, an idea I have for the country" Miss Taitt said in her somewhat I'm-in-the-know manner. "My idea is that we should have a National History and Culture Week, when everyone in every village, every town, and in the capital celebrates being Guianese! We could have concerts, newly written Guianese plays, fresh Guianese poetry and music, Guianese dances . . ."

"And Guianese food," I thought to myself, realising I loved Hindu and Amerindian cookery.

"We should do pageants of our history, display our paintings and carvings . . ." petite, soft spoken, iron-willed Miss Taitt was elaborating. There was a ringing in my ears.

My heart hammered enough to deafen me. Here were the ideas I got into trouble for asking about at Bishops! Here were my ideas properly formed into a national programme being told to me by a woman who'd lived in New York and who thought on a grand scale.

"The musical will be," she was explaining, "about a Guianese canecutter and his Buxton-spice country sweetheart. A dance sequence with graveyard jumbies . . ."

". . . will give you the Willies!" we said in unison and laughed at our ballet joke. How wonderful to feel we were on the same wave-length.

"Newspaper boys, Bookers sales girls, a good-time girl . . ." she explained the characters. "We'll use classical ballet techniques to tell a Guianese love story. You see, a mix of European and Guianese cultures set in an American entertainment form the musical." I couldn't dance on stage for years, I knew that, but in this very moment I'd caught the vision I'd been seeking.

". . . spoken, informally of course, to my friend Dr Cheddi Jagan about History and Culture Week. He's had similar thoughts and he'll propose the idea in the Legislative Council during a debate. That is, when the Opposition is given speaking time." Miss Taitt was referring to the leader of the Opposition party in our Parliament, whom she admired.

"Ah Mona," I reasoned in my pulsating head, "this brilliant idea is not yours alone. The Almighty be praised. It is your classmates' idea. The politicians' and the nation's idea too. You mustn't feel alone any more. Most locals want to be proud Guianese. Not to be Britons with black faces. Not to be white Bishops girls but black Bishops girls seeking knowledge from all over the globe."

It was beginning to dawn on me why this idea frightened the British, who wished us to remain a colony.

"We want complete independence from Britain!" locals had begun chanting at Bourda Green.

"Lunatics! Fanatics!" a newspaper, which preferred the British as our rulers, rubbished them.

"Down with Internal Self Government! We want Independence! Now!"

"Radicals!" cried the police arriving to break up the marches.

"British Guiana after Ghana!" some chanted.

"Disperse! Or face arrest and jail!" the riot police ordered.

"British go home!" union members chanted.

". . . but this colony cannot govern itself!" said influential speakers, with BBC accents, on Mrs Thorne's radio.

"Britain doesn't lose sleep over whether she can govern herself. She thinks freedom is her right. Well, we think freedom is ours too! Be in no doubt, we'll not lose a moment's sleep over being free of Britain!" Spoken by the popular black, Oxford-educated lawyer Forbes Burnham.

"Agitators!" fumed the British Government. Troops flew in from England to 'keep order'.

Local politicians spoke to rousing demonstrations and rallies.

"Dat's right Comrade Leader!" locals cheered them on. "Dat's de truth! Massa-day is over. De English Governor must go!"

"MASSA DAY'S DONE! MASSA DAY'S DONE!" became the catch cry.

"COMMUNISTS!" declared the British.

"Why dey against COMMON-NESS?" local church-goers wondered. "After all, all o' we married people does do common-ness!"

'Wanted' leaders skilfully dodged arrest for disturbing the peace, but how would they continue to voice their opinions with demonstrations and rallies being banned?

"Well, de stricter de government, de wiser de population!" pupils whispered the folk proverb.

"You mean, de shrewder de population," a voice said.

"Amen, just the same!" we agreed, nodding knowingly.

"Was it shattered?" local pupils asked furtively before class.

"Nah! They'd spread sugar bags all around the base. On the ground. It fell on the sacking. We rode past the Law Courts to see it. Before school. Police everywhere!"

"What was the rest of her like?" I whispered.

"OK. Still standing. Majestic!" We fell into each other's arms and laughed soundlessly till the tears came.

"The marble robes are still draped over her marble shoulders. The marble orb's still sitting in her hand!" said Mouth-a-pres-pres, a green eyed Guianese classmate who always was up on the latest gossip. Close mouthed we trooped to our desks. The French mistress entered and we sat absolutely silently, seemingly hard at work translating the adventures of M. Poiret but notes passed excitedly from friend to friend.

In the corridor at morning break, girls whose fathers' troops had flown out to the colony to 'keep order', were wide eyed, pale and shaken having just heard the news. They told us in shocked voices, "Someone's blasted off the head of Queen Victoria. On the marble statute in front of the Law Courts!"

"Horrors! No! Not the Great Queen herself!"

"The rest of the statue is standing . . ." English voices quavered.

"Such majesty! What a tragedy!" We asked po-faced "When? Why?"

"It was on the radio in the staffroom."

"Shocking!" we huffed with straight faces. "Imagine!"

". . . and in front of the Law Courts!"

"Hardly justice!" we spoke in our BBC voices.

"What an absolutely stupid thing for someone to do!" said a voice with a Glaswegian accent. "I can't see the point of it."

"We can!" came a soft chorus of local voices.

"Well," I joined in, speaking in my debater's Properly. "I'm absolutely sure the maaaarvelous troops would neeevah have dreamt of doing that! I mean, it simply would neeevah have crossed their loyal logical minds!" Locals, hands covering their mouths, were battling fits of laughter. Foreign girls avoided comment, but recently arrived third former, Anne, was ready to boil over. Her unusual lips were so startingly red they looked a pretty ruby port and fascinated us locals. A knot of girls milled around us.

"Look, Mona! Don't be so ruddy stupid! If you don't know what to say why don't you just jolly well shut your trap! Of course the troops would never . . ."

". . . but that's what I said!" I cut in. "The troops would neeevah blast away at marble! Good heavens no! They only shoot down flesh and blood. Locals!" I kept on walking.

That vision from Miss Taitt, of blending Guianese and European arts, impelled me to live for ballet. Monday to Friday I paid for and attended Beginners' Class from 4 to 5 p.m. Following on in the next hour I was permitted to observe from my seat the grade classes which Miss Taitt also taught. I scribbled notes. Grade Classes were from 5 to 6 p.m. Later, if I never spoke during classes and made myself invisible, I could learn the Ballet Guiana Company's technique for free from 6 to 7 p.m. Normally boisterous, I managed to become like wallpaper, trying out the steps, turns, positions, combinations, poses, leaps, beats, lunges and port-de-bras way over in the far corner, silently.

When the company carried on into rehearsing a show from 7 to 8 p.m., I learned well but performed poorly the routines my untrained body attempted. It simply required staying out of everybody's way and following the movements of the *corps de ballet* from behind the back line. Other times it was best to squeeze up near the piano which Mr Sam played with a light touch. Not a few times cold stares from others informed me painfully of how not quite pushy but how bare-faced I was to attend fifteen free classes a week by merely asking permission to be there. Ballet was forcing me to cultivate physical strength, stamina, flexibility and a knowledge of technique. In the process I was discovering the value of silence, of invisibility if needed, of watchfulness and of creating my own opportunities.

After a full school day and ballet from 4 to 8 p.m. you'd think I'd be knackered. Miss Taitt, whom we in the Beginners' Class guessed was in her fifties, always tried to appear anything but exhausted after teaching so many classes herself. However, we read in the tense forced smiles and the drooping eyelids what her erect body wished to mask. Slave-tired myself at times, but not every time, I'd trudge six kilometres home and do what homework I could by midnight before falling into a dead-from-drowning sleep. Hunger and fatigue plagued me less when I danced.

At the ballet school's first end-of-year prize-giving, the cup for 'The most outstanding student in the School of Guiana Ballet' was awarded to me. Thinking of myself still as a clumsy beginner this flabbergasted me as much as it did everyone else, because there were in the grades at least two other students of superior natural ability. A particlar Amerindian-and-Portuguese girl impressed us with her terrific Russian back. She'd stand, slide her left leg backwards along the floor, then arch gracefully backwards to rest her head against her left calf. I respected her ability to remember routines and to manage three turns during the musical phrase into which everyone else fitted only one turn. My eyes analysed how she moved, for tips on mastering techniques quickly. Only then would I polish movements with my personal style. I had assumed that she would scoop the prize although she irritated other dancers by showing off, by pushing to the front of the class, and by simply having to be the first

111

dancer attempting new turns across the floor. Her style was athletic while mine was lyrical. My manner was less aggressive then hers and appeared softer, only because I felt less confident. And, ooh! she moved her arms a shade more gracefully than I did. Who needed spectacles to see that she flirted, giggled loudly, and spoke with a fake aristocratic English accent in spite of her humble Guianese background? I noticed all that yet thought well of her, understanding that her struggles as an Amerindian were similar to mine being black. When I told her "I still think you should have won," tears filled her eyes and her chin wobbled. It was the only time she ever allowed us a glimpse beneath her loud cackle and constant smiles.

All the same, here was the first prize that any school itself had ever bestowed on me and the tears settled in my eyes. Earning the respect of very strict Miss Taitt was even more highly valued. Then too, my family understood this trophy when I brought it home. They well knew how to display a silver cup.

Gradually it had become necessary at Bishops to work intently during classes because time was scarce later on. Some homework was even done during the tea breaks and lunch hours, when I borrowed from friends' textbooks I could not afford to buy, to keep on top of things. As a result there was little mixing with other girls. I even tended to race through the school gate promptly at 3.15 p.m. On the plus side, trouble and I parted company once my life revolved around ballet and included the pleasant enough Saturday morning job at Bookers which made it possible.

"You've missed two lunch hour practices for the elocution contest this year. Either you're serious and show up or you drop out and stop wasting my time! No more warnings," the English mistress said quietly. Where was I to find that time? More importantly, should I decide to continue prattling English poetry like an English duck? Winning elocution prizes had counted with the staff when they considered my expulsion. No doubt about it either, that accent gave me the means to defend myself in the verbal jousting which was all part of Bishops life. Still, Keith jeered when he heard me practising.

"Everybody stop what you doing! Don't stupidee yourself! Listen good! Dis girl here can jaw-jaw like de white people! Soooo niiice de white people does even hand she de first prize!"

Claire, who laughed so hard she often wet herself, would fly down the passage-way of our flat, on her way to the toilet, screaming hysterically in 'mock-Properly', "Veeerrry Fuuuuuny Moan-sie!"

"I'll thump both of you!" I'd threaten as they scattered.

Only once had I forgotten myself and spoken Properly with my Christianburg friends who'd said, "Is wha' do you? Who you thinking you is? Don't try talking like no white people to we. You born and grow right here. Not in no England! You never even travel outta dis country past de beacon!"

It had become burdensome to juggle two ways of speaking which clashed if my two different worlds met outside the school grounds. Even Mudsie's wish to impress her customers prompted a scolding. "Is what I can sell you?" I had asked. When the customer had left Mudsie said heatedly, "'Cause we paying for you to get a good education, we ent want you coming outta Bishops talking any old how. You couldda do that without leaving Christianburg. So you just speak Properly, Miss!"

Easter Holidays of 1958 at Christianburg. Midnight. Mummy's Housing Scheme bungalow on Wismar Hill. Hushed excitement. Murmured chat and giggles. Gathered are Mudsie, Mummy and us three children, Auntie Lona and her two kids, Mr Banks who taught with Mummy and about a dozen other family and friends. Grandad who'd retired from his job at Mackenzie Hospital and was home for days on end for the first time in forty years, was also with us. We couldn't have avoided coming home. Olivia was travelling up to see her common-law husband, Shalto. Granny Adrianna had railed against being part of this jiggery-poggery. Clothes, wash tub and all, she had moved out from Mudsie's to live with her daughter Auntie Gladys, until she could calm down again.

We dressed by candle light in white robes, strapped on sandals, then the women added gold jewellery, white head scarves of rich broderie anglaise material and daubed on perfume. Each of the men took up a staff and stood tall and proud, looking defiant and manly. Our company of about twenty walked with ceremonial splendour into the cool midnight air, under a star-sprinkled, rich-black sky, across the sands to the compound of the House of Worship. An orange bonfire that etched the eyes and lives forever on the brain, lit up the enclosed yard. Welcoming us was Shalto in a white caftan, his shaved head swathed, thank goodness, in a huge white turban. Olivia, Miss Ivy, a mother of eight from Essequibo, and a few other families from our district were also there, all dressed in white. They greeted us with embraces. Others dribbled in over the hour.

We guarded the flames, men on one side, women and children on the other. Already turning, roasting and spicing the air was the entire carcase of a lamb on a spit hanging over a separate charcoal cooking fire. Olivia, with an air of authority, took charge of one goat-skin drum, Shalto jerked on to his shoulder the strap of the bigger one. Fat Mr Banks strummed his guitar, a novel addition, and with a sense of decorum, we began to clap, drum, hit home-made calabash shakers and tambourines, sing, sway, wave walking sticks in the air and flash white hankies. We mellowed into the mood after about half an hour of restrained dancing, then Shalto's voice, that of a practised orator in his element, resounded over the drumming.

He flung about his thin black arms in billowing white sleeves, paraded and flourished his carved walking stick and painted colourful word pictures of the dramatic saga, 'The Miracle of

This Night'. How the Almighty, with a strong hand and an outstretched arm, freed our people from the hand of the mighty slave-owner, Pharoah. He, the Almighty, used plagues and the slaying of their first born to free His people. He took us by way of the Red Sea where He drowned Pharaoh's Army and all his chariots. We were free people on our way to 'The Promised Land'. Shalto's voice soared and fell, geysered up and cascaded down. It was by turns silky soft and raven raucous, persuasive and compelling. Though his English had errors of grammar, his style as a storyteller was the finest I had ever experienced. His gold teeth glistened in the firelight and beads of sweat sparkled on his forehead. We listened spellbound to a story magician. This Passover night was near enough to the Christian festival of Easter, and thus was during the Bishops school holidays. We were celebrating Passover because our most closely guarded secret was that we regarded ourselves as Jews.

By 2 a.m., having been captivated and uplifted by all that marvellous blood and thunder, we'd relax and get into the real festivities. Adults sliced straight off the spit, finger-frying-hot lamb and dropped it on to our palm over which had been spread a flat, floppy Indian wheat bread called roti, made without leaven. Mummy would ladle over spoonfuls of stewed bitter corylla known as Japanese bitter melon. We'd wash the meal down with sips of wickedly heady rice wine made weeks ago by Mudsie. No one ever appeared drunk from it but I came close, more than a few times. There'd be fruit cake made without leaven by Mudsie, pone and tarts from other families, home made guava cheese, pineapple drink and Mackintosh toffees. The air, warmed by leaping orange flames and white shooting sparks, wafted into our nostrils. It was a fragrant blend of Evening-in-Paris perfume, food aromas, burnt lamb fat, coconut oil which had been rubbed on to our feet to pamper the skin, perspiration, rice wine and pine-wood smoke.

Everyone wore smiles of contentment and camaraderie, caught

up on who had which job and who was sailing to live in London. The kids told each other jokes. The women eyed each other's gold jewellery and noted who was expecting another baby. Parents boastfully complained about how expensive it was to keep kids in Georgetown schools. The men lined up jobs for each other's sons. Sadly, as the flames died and the mosquitoes returned to bite, our dancing, drumming and telling The Story of This Night would cease. Then, as the crowing of village birds bugled through the chilly air, we'd melt out of the yard as silently as the river's flow before day-clean came, and with it the possibility of the public recognising us.

"Mudsie, is why Granny Adrianna don't want to keep Passover?"

"She belongs to the Brethren Church."

"I know. But why she always calling what we do jiggery poggery?" I undressed out of my Passover whites at Mummy's bungalow.

"Everybody calls whatever African people do to worship jiggery poggery," she fumed. "Or they call it 'working obeah' or 'practising voodoo' or 'dabbling with spirits' or 'heathen blindness' or some other stupidness. They think the only holy way to worship is to belong to the Anglicans or the Catholics, or like that." Mudsie jerked off her rich white headscarf. It hit and cracked the glass chimney of Mummy's kerosene lamp.

"But we never let anyone know we have a different religion. And you make me shut up about it even to our friends," I complained. "I couldn't tell even Sister Dolly why I didn't want to eat garlic pork, or callaloo and crab soup or her friend's iguana curry." The bustle around us hushed, showing respect for Mudsie.

In a tired, patient voice Mudsie said, "Life is precious, picknee. Worshipping in the Jewish way is precious, me chile. Not so long ago the Police wouldda marched in, wouldda break up the drums and wouldda hanged all o' we. The charge wouldda been 'practising voodoo'." Mudsie was panting softly so she sat on the living room couch. "The Hindus and Moslems, the Chinese and the Putagee . . ."

"Portuguese," I corrected.

". . . worship in their own way. Their religion is legal. Their god even looks like them. But our people? The British outlaw our people's worship. They say we got to keep to the white people's religion! We gotta even worship a white-faced Jesus. White faced! De white people even paint over their Jesus to look likka them. But, how could Jesus from Nazareth, from Zion next door to Africa, from dat part o' the world near Jordan, be white and not a brown-skinned man? You tell me that!" I had never given it a thought. The realisation shocked me.

"So, our people, we learn to live with secrets. But . . . ah ha! That's how we can worship. In secret. And what the British people don't know about they can't destroy." Then she nodded at me and drew off her white robe gently. We continued to disrobe silently, lost in thought.

Secrets, I must confess, felt like having a heavy basket of groceries on my head while trying to swim. Secrets about my religion, about Granny Adrianna's farm, my father leaving our family penniless, my loathing of Bishops, my distrusting Shalto and Olivia, and worst of all, about my growing distance from my own mother. To whom could I speak? Although guarded in what I said, I needed to talk with him.

"Dear Dad, . . ." excitedly written letters flew to Wembley in England to his semi-detached home (What is that Dad?) and returned with photographs of a stout, dark, middle-aged man in thick woollen winter clothes. He looked like an older Keith!

"What he mean that this is a picture of 'the baby of the family'?" I asked Claire when we'd returned to Georgetown with Olivia to resume school. The letters had been waiting for us.

"Haven't the foggiest," she said, both of us staring at a photo of only our dad and a car in front of a brick house.

117

"He said he used to work as a crane operator in Glasgow," I read his letter, "on the docks when he first arrived in '46 to help rebuild the Mother Country, after the war."

"Umm humm," Claire said, putting away her homework and preparing for bed.

"Said he got pneumonia after his first English winter. Broke his health for good, he said."

"What, he can't walk now, or what?" Claire snorted. I motioned her to speak quietly in case Olivia were listening in the other bedroom.

"Dunno. Lived near St Martin-in-the-Fields for a while," he said. "What's that?"

"Search me!" Claire was putting curlers into her straightened hair. The pretty thing! Those long eyelashes and that tiny gap between her front teeth! Like cricketer Garfield Sobers' smile. I waved the second photo in the letter under her nose and she was instantly inquisitive. Keith had flaked out atop his sheet without tucking his mosquito net over his bed. They'd eat him alive unless one of us did the netting for him.

"She good looking nuh?" I said, photo held up to the light.

"Fair skinned, straight hair, plump, short, umm . . . OK looking," Claire scrutinised the photo.

"She clothes look expensive," I offered. "Dad says she's a Guianese. Related to a big Georgetown lawyer family."

"What she name?" Claire let me scan the letter. I announced, "Iris. Like Granny Adrianna's youngest child, Auntie Iris. Nice eh?"

"She got a second name?" the tone was decidedly sharp.

"Why you so hog-stylish, Claire? She is a Mahadoo. Good family."

"What else?" Claire continued to put in curlers but was obviously curious.

"How old she look like?" I pushed the photo before her eyes.

118

"Must be 'bout forty, nugh? Got a big behind, but it's tidy looking," was Claire's verdict.

"She is a worker, you know Claire, a seamstress." I read a bit more.

"At Norman Hartnell's establishment. He, um my father, er, Edmund, er Dad says she sews the seed pearls and beading on to the ball gowns." Claire looked blankly so I had to explain, "Norman Hartnell. Queen Elizabeth's dressmaker! You know."

"Eh!Eh!" The astonishment flew out involuntarily.

"You think they well off?" I asked Claire.

"Haven't the foggiest. And why de France you bothering me with those stupid photos? I tired. Turn off the light. I want to go to sleep," she snapped. I heard the catch in her voice. I thought it best to put away the letter with the photo of Dad, his car and his house, and the second snapshot of his woman companion of umpteen years. Without a word we dropped Keith's mosquito net over his bed and tucked the ends under the mattress, but not before I'd noticed tear drops falling on the back of Claire's brown hand.

"Don't ever show those to Mummy either," my head hammered my heart, "she'll behave like a first-class fire-ass!" Unwillingly I'd gained yet another secret.

Fifteen

Silly with joy! That's how I'd become at the news that Olivia was leaving us for good. It happened in a roundabout way. The congregation led by Shalto, had visited the capital for a day of demonstrations to demand that the government recognise our faith. Our families had paraded in our Passover whites with placards reading, "RECOGNISE US!" and "PUT US ON THE NATIONAL REGISTER OF RELIGIONS!" As it was midterm break Claire, Keith and I had swelled the meagre ranks of adults chanting and marching on the pavement. 'Collar n' tie' clerks in the pillared building which housed the Treasury and the Legislative Council, our parliament, stared with amusement at us beyond the wrought iron fence of their compound. Nothing came of our efforts beside an invitation for the men to troop inside and present their written submission to a white official. I had seen enough of demonstrations to know that none of our congregation understood how to get what Shalto wanted from the authorities. While the women and children waited on the pavement outside, one Bishops 'old girl' who'd walked importantly down to read the placards through the fence was startled to see me. She spoke archly through her nose.

"Hello Mona. I recognise you. You come into the Treasury every September to collect your scholarship book allowance from me, don't you now? You're in the same class as my niece, Marguerite. She talks about you. Often. Very often." She leaned her lean, brown face with finely chiselled features close to the fence and spoke elegantly, Properly, in a Bishops' whisper. "Well, I hope nobody else recognises you! Or who can say which bigwig might hear about this and invite Bishops to send you packing! That'll be that, won't it?" She turned on her terribly high heels, and I watched her slight, well dressed figure retreat as her heels tapped a steely message in the concrete path to the Treasury.

Months later, Olivia announced a future addition to her family and her wish to be near Shalto. I danced on my morning walk to Bishops. Brickdam was suddenly fascinating. There for the world's admiration was a towering cannon ball tree, its powerfully perfumed giant red flower spicing the air four blocks away from its place, in front of St Andrew's church manse. It bore brown fruit the size of cannon balls, directly on its massive brown trunk.

Five minutes later my eyes scanned the gingerbread trim on the multi-storied white colonial home of black film actor Robert Adams. I'd seen him in a movie, *Man of Two Worlds.* Now he'd returned from London a little famous! Across the road from the Adams' house was the small, cream-painted, wooden Smith's Congregational Church of the Vreed-en-Hoop slave rebellion. Two minutes later, where Brickdam meets Camp Street, massive Brickdam Cathedral loomed. I remember attending mass there while boarding with Catholic Aunt Carrie. A few blocks further up I sauntered past imposing Brickdam Police Headquarters. Two of my uncles worked there, Uncle Basil, a big wheel in Traffic and Uncle Eustace in forensic photography, for which he had been awarded the OBE. They were my father's brothers whom I knew by sight but with whom I had no contact. Just before arriving at Bishops the road took a stately circle around St George's Anglican Cathedral, said to be the tallest wooden building in the world. We sang there once a year at Commemoration Service, conducted by the Dean of Georgetown, with the Governor in attendance. Our voices soaring in uplifting anthems, bounced clearly off the polished wood panels in the cathedral roof. Ahead, up the avenue, was Bishops. Sweating from the brisk morning walk I'd greet school life with a headful of visions.

Joy was mingled with sadness over Claire's O level exam results. Not a pass in a single subject. She left Georgetown to begin working at Ituni, a mining town beyond Christianburg. Our flat, it was decided, would be given up. Keith and I would continue High School, lodging in a recently built flat below the first floor of Aunt Lydia Maud's house of memories. I'd homing-pigeoned to nest eight years later at Durban and Cemetery Roads.

"Well, what y'all doing at school?" graceful Miss Mae small-talked when Mummy delivered us there. I liked her tiny home immediately.

"Keith win scholarship to St Stanislaw's College, so he there since September '57," Mummy said quietly, but I caught the pride in her smile.

Eye-sweeping the highly polished wooden sitting-room floor, I moved my gaze up to Miss Mae's easy chairs with fresh, clean covers and along to a cabinet with crystal clinking as you walked past it. China and silver were on display and so, oh Lawd, was a big Pye radio. My mind was continents away.

"Speak up nuh chile, you lost you mouth?" Mummy was urging me but I said nothing because I hadn't heard the question.

"Well then, tell me what you taking this year," Miss Mae coaxed softly.

"I studying to take the Oxford and Cambridge O level exams," I said in Guianese and saw her frown, so shifted gears into Properly.

"So June next year, 1960, I'll sit the exams in History, Botany, English Literature and English Language, Biology, Geography and Home Economics."

"Why you not studying to take de Mathematics?" She was quick to notice the omission.

"I can do the work but I can't stand that teacher for a year."
My frankness earned another frown.

"But everybody needs de Maths," Miss Mae countered,
glancing shrewdly at me as a crocodile squints at a monkey.

"I hear you does de Ballet," Miss Mae took another tack.

"Every schoolday from 4 to 8 p.m."

"You know any white people's children at the ballet school?"
she continued.

"Oh, Melanie Thompson, Maura Milliken . . ."

"I used to work for her family, de Millikens," Miss Mae tried
to find a link between us. She mentioned 'de white people dem
who have they children going to Bishops', families for whom
she'd been a cook, housemaid and nanny. Telling her something
admirable about each girl she'd cared for did the trick. She was
pleased to have me as a boarder. There'd be moments later to
fill her in on my Bookers job and elocution training times.

Keith shared the men's bedroom with Miss Mae's father Paa-
pa and her saga-boy brother Uncle Bomb, who'd made and
squandered a spectacular fortune in the Mazaruni gold fields.
Keith's eyes sized up the situation but his tongue took no liberties.
He just washed his face in little boy charm. This, as always,
won over the ladies. Miss Mae, we knew from the way she smiled
at Keith, would dote on him as Mudsie, Granny Adrianna,
Mummy and Claire always had.

I shared the bedroom-cum-sewing salon with a fanatically neat
Miss Mae and her only child Enid, a savvy seamstress. Twenty-
seven-ish, smashingly good looking, brown eyed Enid dressed
like a film star in body-hugging garments that window-dressed
her stunning figure. Her clients were wealthy socialite families
who brought along pictures of fashionable French dresses which
Enid then sewed without ever having a pattern. This impressed
me more than a little, since Enid's schooling had ended before
she sat her High School Certificate exam. Fun loving, Enid
dazzled her admirers but hadn't yet found Mr Right, so she'd

spent the last decade seeing and being seen at the races and at exclusive civil service parties. Enid was as sociable as her mother was shy.

The first dinner cooked by Miss Mae convinced us that we had fallen on our feet.

". . . but, pork, shell fish (like shrimps), and blood which you use to make black pudding, we don't eat. Is we 'Kinna'," I said, using the African word for a food taboo. Miss Mae accepted this without comment and served us different meals. Weekly her radio poured a wealth of regular entertainment into our previously spartan lives. Our minds stretched beyond British Guiana as we enjoyed the *Saturday Hit Parades*, the BBC's *Navy Lark* comedy, request programmes, *Voice of America Jazz*, calypsoes, cricket test matches from all over the Caribbean, BBC dramas, quiz shows, talent contests, BBC World News, American boxing matches, *London Calling the Caribbean*, interviews with American celebrities and soaps. Life flourished now there was more than study to it. Miss Mae complained only about our untidy habits, but Keith grew plumper and I more contented. My brother and I became good buddies. I called him M'sieur Renee after the hero of a radio soap we listened to regularly and he keeled over laughing at my ballet frame and renamed me Boney Yard or Bones for short. We learned to share with each other about school and friends but I strapped my worries to my chest alone.

Miss Mae's favourite soap opera was of Uncle Bomb's stupidity.

"When he found dat gold, oh Laaawd! He had so much money he give away thousands o' dollars to he new-faced friends. And spend de rest entertaining gold fields women. He didn't study to say, 'Let me give some gold to me own family. Let me help me 'things bad' sister.' Now Bomb ent got a cent, where is all he fair weather friends den? So you-all must remember to help you-all family first when you-all get up in the world. Y'hear?"

To us though, Uncle Bomb's life was more like a roller-coaster adventure than a disaster. Good times and bad sat on his huge, gentle black frame easily, lightly. We were fascinated by the jokes he told of his gold fields' hardships.

Things went swimmingly from September '59 until February '60 when Mummy failed to pay our board for two months running, without a letter of explanation. Desperately hand to mouth herself, Miss Mae bundled us on to a launch with firm instructions to remain at home until past debts were settled and future accounts guaranted.

"I only want a certificate with at least one pass on it," my mind repeated in rhythm to the motor of Mr Oxley's launch.

Having to forfeit at least one month's study in the final months of my exam year left me panicked, but I knew well enough to put on a happy face. My voice warbling like a kiss-ka-dee's when Mummy greeted us, you'd have thought nothing was amiss.

"What happened?" I put it gently after dinner.

"Nothing. I just didn't have the money." Mummy had rehearsed her lines.

"Why didn't you?" It was a plea dressed up like a question.

"How the hell you mean 'Why didn't I'? Who the France is you to question me? I don't have to answer to no child of mine!"

So there! I had Mummy's no-answer! We both were in a simmering, polite fury.

"Put that in yer pipe and smoke it!" joked Keith. He and I spluttered into respectful laughter balanced on the edge of tears. Though, who'd have needed spectacles to have seen where the money had gone? I could have foretold this two bedroom bungalow years ago without being a see-far-ian. I knew that the community was funding their advisor-man as if he were a priest. They housed him and his family. Shalto enjoyed his comfortable living made possible by the congregation's gifts of money, every month. He repaid his followers by showing them dazzling visions of expensive achievements, like house building.

125

They all took his advice. Mummy looked as poor now as a fruit bat after the banana harvest.

Similarly, Mudsie's cash box in the breadshop held shillings not dollar notes. The two-storied house itself had stood up well to daily baking in the sun but repainting on the outside was sorely needed. Mildred, our servant of my childhood years, had been let go. The damask table cloths spread for special occasions, were now stained and well darned. None had been imported recently from England to replace them. Mudsie spent the time between serving customers, seated at her treadle sewing machine, embroidering blue birds of happiness and English flowers on pillowcases, handtowels, tablecloths and sheets which had all been fashioned from bleached flourbags. Most telling, in the kitchen of this woman who adored cooking, was the state of her pots. The rubber ring in the lid of her pressure-cooker had perished but had not been replaced, so all the steam escaped during cooking.

There was clearly no alternative but to propose the plan I'd hatched on my river cruise to Christianburg.

"Mummy, could we bake cakes and tarts after you come home from school and have me sell them door to door on Wismar Hill everyday? We'll more than make the money in a month," my voice kiss-ka-dee-ed.

"You'll do that?" Mummy was incredulous. Bishops girls never hawked goods door to door like uneducated market mortals.

"That's how Mudsie started her business and . . ." my explanation began.

"Hand wash hand makes hands clean." Mummy's proverb welcomed my co-operation.

Far from feeling humiliated I enjoyed greeting familiar home folks who'd bought Mudsie's bread for years. They spoke to me as, "Miz Nelson grand-picknee. Chile, how you do?"

"Mudder Harris, ah deh. Nutting ent comin 'gainst me. How Ullrick and Pylee and Daddy H?"

"Dey fine Chile. How come you home? You ent at Bishops no more?" Mrs Harris would enquire.

"Ah going back at month end, but at the moment 'paisa na baa'," I'd admit to my penniless state, speaking broken Hindu.

"Well, finding de money fo dat school would give anyone a big goodee!" she'd sympathise. Such warmth was mine because I spoke Guianese and wasn't 'great-up'.

Returned to Georgetown Miss Taitt found me sobbing softly in the dressing room when she locked up for the night.

". . . so I need some way of paying my board. I can't rely on my parents. I'll have to give up ballet." I bit back the sobs. Ballet dancers didn't carry on in public.

"I'll think about it and we'll see tomorrow." She looked shaken.

Morning breaktime the next day the debating mistress summoned me to the Bishops staff room door.

"Now what's this all about? What's this I hear? We think you ought to speak to the headmistress."

"I could never shame my family . . . Miss Harris will believe black people don't look after their children." Dry-eyed my heart was pounding.

"Well, I'll be discreet but you must speak up. I'll arrange an appointment for you with Miss Harris. Lunch hour's fine?"

Molly-the-Mop Harris was neutral, controlled, official and quietly spoken. Her piercing grey-blue eyes surveyed my stick-thin frame. My tie was like a piece of shredded rope and my skirt was faded. My socks were grubby as they were my only pair, but my blouse was clean but patched. My teeth were brown from decay.

"We've been able to buy a second hand tie till you get yours. The hat suppliers are experimenting with a new weave of straw and would welcome your consenting to be their guinea-pig. Do tell them how it wears during the year." The voice betrayed no emotion.

"The Science Department also needs a lab assistant to set out equipment and chemicals for the following day and to clear away each afternoon after school. The pay is thirty dollars a month. Do let me know tomorrow if you wish the position."

I said a respectful "thank you" and tore off to the cloak room. I bolted myself in a cubicle and did not come out until my eyes were dry. Would I make a botch of putting out chemicals and equipment which I neither knew of nor used? Needing the money wasn't reason enough to take a job I felt I couldn't do.

"I've observed you," said a decidedly tired looking Miss Taitt after I'd had danced in my grade class. "I'm proposing a deal with certain conditions." She was less friendly now. Formal. Distant.

"You can teach the beginners' ballet class from 4 to 5 p.m., Monday to Friday, and I'll pay you thirty dollars a month." Had I just heard that? My thighs were quivering.

"For you to teach the beginners competently, I am requiring that you attend your grade class, the company classes and the company rehearsals every school night. That means you must attend fifteen classes a week. You've been doing this by choice already. Now it is compulsory and all . . . er . . . free of charge." There was no ballet mistress' smile as at ordinary times, this was a business discussion.

"Thank you very much Miss Taitt. I'll do it." I managed not to leap or shout in agreeing to this soul-soaring offer.

"Not at all. I'll expect you tomorrow," she said with the ballet dancer's smile now on, bulb-bright.

"One moment Mona. Please show me a lesson plan of the barre and floor exercises which you'll use as warm-ups in the first half hour. Here's a book if you're not sure of the French spelling." It was a Royal Ballet Company volume on technique, with lavish photographs of well trained, gorgeous dancers in correct and incorrect positions. I'd often poured over it.

"Then, list the combinations, turns across the room, adages, jettés and final jumps and stretches for the second half hour." I gulped although I well knew the lesson format and repertoire.

"Mention the music you hope Mr Sam will play. Variety is important." The rest was lost to my shocked scrambled brain ". . . lyricism in your floor work, ballon in your jettés . . . cover space . . . use the diagonals . . . On my table, fifteen minutes before class begins." Dumb struck, I appeared politely silent.

"Oh, there's a small run in your tights. You'll fix it before tomorrow, won't you? And, er, what about perfume, a bow in your hair, lipstick and nail varnish?" She flashed that dazzling professional smile and remembering myself, I plastered on mine too.

Madness! Why take this job? Go back and tell her to put this job where the monkey put the nut! A minimum of twenty classes taught for thirty dollars! Slave labour. I'm saving her from exhaustion too. And the writing up, when will I do that!

"You know, God didn't make no hard work until after He'd made black people!" Granny Adrianna's voice recited the proverb in my head. "It won't kill you. Do it!" her voice seemed to command.

Happiness! Why not take it? You'll do it better than the science job. You could be part of BG's dance history, Bones!

I took it. Dropping botany lightened the exam load to six subjects. The Bookers wages I had used as fees for grade classes bought instead working clothes for Saturday's job, uniform items for Bishops, ballet gear and a sturdy second hand ladies bike paid for in three instalments. Cycling zinged me to school and breezed me six tired kilometres home after ballet by 8.30 p.m. Miss Taitt's ballet wages paid the board to Miss Mae on time and left five dollars a month for keeping things afloat. It was never enough. Studies were managed, just.

"Well chile! God don't close a door without He open a window," Miss Mae commented drily when we realised that

129

Mummy would no longer be paying my keep. As a working high school pupil, I had seen my love, ballet, become my life-line.

The school's notice to the parents said that the fifth form O level G.C.E. exam fees of ten dollars a subject were due at month-end.

"Sixty dollars. Urgent. Please Dad. A bank draft. By the 30th. I'm begging you. The first time in my life. Mummy doesn't have it. No fees . . . no O level certificate! I can pass. I'm sure. Studied for this since I was twelve. I'm nearing seventeen now. I've worked like Billy-O. Sacrificed. Please . . ." So near and yet so far. Days skimmed by. No reply from Wembley. I became numb.

No! I will not recite the 23rd Psalm. No! I will not say any Psalms of Hope. No! I will not sing Miss Bacchus' 'Thanks be to God'. No! I'm not going to beg You, Almighty! No! I don't think much of parents, earthly or heavenly, who won't provide for their children when I know they can. They should be tried as criminals! And Yes! I will recite the T. S. Elliot poem we had to practise as an elocution exercise.

> Where is there an end of it, the soundless wailing,
> The silent withering of autumn flowers
> Dropping their petals and remaining motionless;
> Where is there an end to the drifting wreckage,
> The prayer of the bone on the beach, the unprayable
> Prayer at the calamitous annunciation?
>
> There is no end, but addition; the trailing
> Consequence of further days and hours,
> While emotion takes to itself the emotionless
> Years of living among the breakage
> Of what was believed in as the most reliable . . .

Cycling on a one-way boulevard beside the Civic Gardens, the after-school sun's glint on an object at the road's edge caught my eye. My bike, Calypso, was hastily propped on its stand and I belted back to snatch up the yellow and black plastic object. There was no other person in sight. I shoved the fist sized change purse down my blouse into my bra and sped off. Secretly, in the ballet school's cloak room I sat and stared at it.

"Unzip the purse. Count it," my mind commanded. "Eh? Sixty dollars! Count it once more."

I faced the beginners' ballet class with a round bulky object clearly outlined against my left breast. Who would chance losing this fortune by leaving it in the dressing room? Let the class snigger. Let Gora Singh die laughing! Look, do I have to put up with this raging debate in my head right now. *It's month end, so it must be somebody's entire month's salary. Take it to the Police, sweet Miss Perfect here is going to run a photofinish race with Jesus Christ! True. She'll do the righteous thing! It's the hand of fate that's put it into your hand. Hand it over to your Uncle Basil at Brickdam. Can't you hear them screaming when they find it's lost? How would you like that to happen to you? Or to your mother? The Lord gives and the Lord takes away. Blessed be the name of the Lord. Thou shalt not covet.*

"Gora Singh! And the rest of the class! Perhaps you can control your laughter long enough to show me six soutenu turns properly across the floor. Now!"

No letter came from Wembley. On the final day for paying, although it was a sweltering equatorial afternoon, my body felt freezing cold as Miss Lall took the money and I gripped the receipt for sixty dollars' exam fees.

Keith, believe me, if I could tell you this secret it would answer again the riddle you'd put to me. "When do you feel like ice in the middle of a bread oven?"

Months afterwards Dad's money arrived. My eyes were at last tested, and sorely needed bat wing spectacles bought. Thanks flowed to my father like monsoon rains on to rice fields, but

131

my words on the aerogramme hid exactly what had been paid for. No point in letting Dad imagine I had been 'de duck gettin a pondful to swim in rather than de chicken begging for a beakful to drink.'

Mudsie agreed with what I had written when I told her all later, secretly, on a quick trip home. Then why did I still feel uncomfortably like a thief and a liar?

"Is just that my father doesn't support me regularly," I was saying to Mudsie. "Why should I have to tell my own father I desperately need money for things like toilet soap and toothpaste and shoe polish? Can't he understand that I need shoes, clothes, money for the dentist?"

"Picknee, the man in heaven don't understand what the man in hell going through," she voiced the Guianese saying.

"I can't stomach telling him that I'm poor. I can't beg . . ."

"Tell me something I don't know!" Mudsie mumbled in agreement.

"He might send money for an emergency if I grovel. That's why I don't want him to imagine I made up an emergency. Or else he won't help next time. See? But finding that money and paying the exam fees was . . . was awful."

"The rain you pray for, for planting" Mudsie sighed,

". . . brings mosquitoes with it, as well," I finished the proverb. Though never one for hugging, Mudsie said caressingly, "What else you couldda done, picknee? What else you couldda done?" Then her crochet hook continued to dip expertly back and forth, creating a lace edging for one of Granny Adrianna's flourbag petticoats. We sat silently waiting for customers.

Later, my feet walked without directions from me, into Mudsie's backgarden. Thank heavens we still owned the land. Sitting alone in the grass near to the granadilla vine which grew on a pergola, I looked at the coconut tree which had been planted after Keith was born, swaying by the outhouse. Over there was the chicken coop with stringy old, few-feathered birds. They sometimes disappeared into the stewpots of gamblers who drank rum and played dominoes all day at the Men's Club next door. The men's inventive swearing, regarded as the honey which sweetened their game, drifted over to me as they played. Near my feet ants scurried to their holes carrying huge sections of leaves many times their body weight. Marabunta wasps flew back and forth. Midges and mosquitoes bit from time to time. Burnt-orange fruits of the bromilliad plants in the mango trees caught my eye. An avocado thudded to the ground in the vegetable garden. Was I really home? Could I ever confide to Granny Adrianna that I'd told the Almighty what a toad I'd felt He was? What had happened to me at Bishops? My family had wanted Bishops to change me, but did they understand the kind of changes I'd undergo?

Hugging my knees allowed the sun to hammer relentlessly down on my arms. I knew from its glare and from the crisp shapes of the laundry on the palings to my right, that its heat beat down with more intensity than Mudsie's oven. Yet my body, dew-grass-mornin' cold, continued to shiver. After a good half hour, mahogany arms stinging from sun burn, perspiration trickling down my temple, body tingling but shaking no more, I felt whole again. I heard a wonderfully magical bit of swearing from next door. Then, throwing back my head I laughed and laughed and laughed at nothing in particular.

Sixteen

Exam fever. Two months to go. We crammed, answered old exam papers, reviewed the year's unintelligible notes, tested each other, recited lists, listened intently to the teachers' answers and slept badly. The History and Geography mistress offered Fifths free coaching for eight Saturday mornings. I half-regretted needing to sell tots' shoes on Saturday at Bookers, with everyone saying, "The room's always packed. Reeks. Deodorant, hair pomade and lipstick. We go over everything!" Including who's wearing a ponytail, jeans, which were all the rage, or two can-cans under their Rock-'n-roll flared skirt, I bet. France! I wanted to go to Saturday classes if only to wear something other than work clothes or the Bishops uniform. Not that I owned anything else.

A few girls became religious. Cigarette butts appeared in the school's toilet bowls. Granny Adrianna wrote me the only letter I'd ever received from her, which began not surprisingly:

> Bless the Lord, O my soul,
> And all that is within me
> Bless His Holy name!

Thin and placid, perhaps because of weeks of utter tiredness, it was small wonder I practised my exam questions only by speaking what I planned to write, rather than by actually penning each essay. Extremely tense, my moon rain stopped altogether.

One week before exams my punctured cycle tube was at the bike shop being patched. Trudging home after ballet with dance gear, text books and sewing bulging in a cheap suitcase, my leg thumped against the cardboard lid. The catch suddenly sprang apart. Books cascaded out of the suitcase, littering the pavement. My crisp, pink, floral cotton dress which exhibited perfect sewing for the Home Ec exam floated gracefully down into the stinking muddy drainage canal on Durban Street. Small fish and muck flew everywhere when the dress was pulled out and shaken violently. Mud speckles threatened to cost me my Home Ec certificate. What was I going to do now? I couldn't recut and resew the dress perfectly in seven days.

Repacking only the books, memory surfaced. "What you wantta be when you grow up?" Mummy was persuading me to confide to her that year after we'd boarded with Aunt Lydia Maud.

"I wantta be a worker like Auntie Gladys." The buried dream of my ten year old heart having been unearthed, it had breathed, swayed, and swirled with magical genie-like liveliness. Workers, dressmaking wizards like Auntie Gladys and Enid, cut complicated creations without patterns, day in day out.

"No, you don't want to be no worker!" consternation had embroidered Mummy's fuming. "I sew frocks after teaching at school all day, and workers don't make no proper money. Not a bit of it! You is to be a doctor or a lawyer! You hear me, chile? Black people must have ambition!" Her hurled reprimand had seemed to thud upon and steam-roller over my fragile, tender-precious dream. In reality the genie couldn't be touched. Sitting in the ceiling above our heads it had mocked Mummy's manoeuvre. Silently I had promised myself, "No matter what she, Mummy, says, I'll still be a worker. But I'll sew my own clothes."

Seven years later, elated, I was sewing the exam garment of that bright, defiant ambition. So when it was fished up with trench moss, thick black mud and cock-a-bullies, would I hesitate?

135

Racing home to Miss Mae I left my books, hung up the stinking garment outside to dry, jogged two miles to Janet Jones' home and asked to speak to her father. My polite chats with Janet after the day of my first detention for shouting at her, might now make a difference. Offering the olive branch of, "Janet, can I lend you my book? Borrowed it from the American Embassy Library at lunch time. Its fascin . . . interesting," had led to wary chats between us over the years. That's how I'd learnt that her family knew the examiner of the Home Ec exam. A white nun from St Joseph's Convent High School. All the white people knew each other, or so it seemed to us locals. At this late hour, explaining my plight to Mr Jones my mind argued that he would neither believe nor help me.

". . . could you please . . . um . . . explain to the nun . . . er . . . the examiner . . . about the dress . . . about . . . um . . . what happened tonight? Could she please judge the dress on workmanship and not look at the mud? I'll try to brush out as much as I can . . . cheap material. The colours will run no matter how much salt I put in the water . . . No . . . I daren't wash it . . . it'll look dreadful. Yes. I'm sure of that. Why? Er . . . Um . . . I just know. My great-grandmother is a washerwoman and I help her." I had said it pretty much as it had been rehearsed while jogging over.

"I'll see what I can do," was all he would say. Janet and her mother looked at me silently from their living room as I stood at their front door without being invited in. Still, my heart was grateful and hopeful as I half-ran the two miles home.

"Would I, though, have helped anyone who'd snapped off my child's head?" I pondered.

"You had a jumping nerve! What possessed you! The blessed cheek of it!" the debating mistress spewed razor grass at me at the staffroom door next morning break. "It's not as if you knew Mr Jones or if he knew you! What an utterly presumptious thing to have done! You'd better learn to pull in your horns my girl! And promptly!" The shredding I got still skirted the issue. The unspoken outrage was at my daring to speak to a white man of enormous influence, myself. Normally the school was asked to handle such problems. But Bishops had no obligation to do anything you asked if the principal didn't wish to. Once the problem had been placed with the school it was considered improper for a pupil to do anything about it herself, even when the school refused to act. I had no wish to rely on Bishops because I couldn't be sure Molly would think that asking for consideration was 'proper'. Worse, asking Bishops for help made me feel like a nuisance once again.

"I haven't parents who could have asked for me, Miss," I began, wondering what was the polite thing to admit to and what would be disloyal to my family to disclose. "And you yourself told me I have to speak up. My father's in Wembley, in England. My mother's at Wismar. My guardian is too afraid to ask a favour of anyone, black or white. What should I have done, Miss?" Confused, I still kept my demeanour respectful.

"I see. You aren't . . . er, living with your family?" I shook my head.

"Haven't, in term time, since I've been at Bishops. Or for most o' my life." Should I apologise or remain standing there or slink off for a sniffle in the cloakroom? Unsure, I stood ballerina-poised like Miss Taitt, faking confidence. My head remained high but sweat poured down my inner arms soaking into my shirt sleeves.

She said in her gentlest tone ever used with me, "Good heavens Mona! No one knew this. All these years. You're somewhat, er, how shall I put it? . . . on your own."

Exam week saw it all. Girls broke down during their paper. Others rode silently home. After midnight-cramming, one friend slept in and took her seat an hour late. Popular Marguerite, a talented artist, arrived on Friday afternoon all geared up for her Friday morning art exam. We all ached for her. One white pupil caught with the French verbs scribbled blue on her pink palms received a look that could kill from the exam invigilator. However, the woman knew better than to dare to confiscate the pupil's paper. Some girls who knew the answers didn't write them because they weren't sure that this was what those big words in the questions actually meant. A few bright classmates went blank with fear, completed the two hour paper within an hour and stumbled out weeping.

"Discuss the advantages of central heating over open fire heating," the English language paper invited me to do in Equatorial South America. Should I write a rude note telling the examiner that not only are we eight degrees at the most from the Equator, but that our scorching coast is below sea level and needs sea walls to prevent flooding? There must be an essay topic I could write on. "Advise a friend how to open and use a cheque account." Pardon? I'd seen English postal money orders from Dad, but a cheque? What, in any case, was a cheque account? This exam was not just testing my knowledge of how to use the English language but my knowledge of English culture. Ah well.

Julius Caesar, the Shakespearian question in the Literature exam, was answered with a wealth of quotes and phrases written exactly as the English mistress had expressed them. I had crammed, or rather, memorised the lot. Then I tackled the novel, E. M. Forster's *A Passage to India*. Set in India at the time the sub-continent was agitating for independence, it was not unlike our colony in 1960. The Moslem pupils at Bishops frequently felt they were the relatives of one of the principal characters in the story, so we had enjoyed the novel to a point. During the exam it was as obvious to me as the skin that I sat in, that I had understood the novel imperfectly. True, I knew that whatever this Indian man had been accused of doing to that

English woman, alone with him in a dark cave, would have been dreadfully shocking and coarse. Was it . . . one didn't use certain words at Bishops. Our prim mistress had been coy about exactly what Dr Aziz was supposed to have done and we'd learnt from the evasive answers when to stop asking awkward questions. The accusations were withdrawn during the trial because the deed hadn't really occurred anyway. The woman had had an hallucination, whatever that too was. So, hoping for the best I wrote all the vague words the teacher had used, feeling I couldn't go wrong that way. This was not the time to fume over Bishops choosing to teach us a novel while refusing to make clear to us what the conflict in the story was about.

The poetry section of the Literature paper seemed a gift. I'd spent hours with the elocution group, looking closely at what words meant and the disciplined magic of their use. The other exams, History, Biology and Geography, were neither a breeze nor a terror but Home Economics made me anxious. Each of us had prepared different menus. I wasn't sure if I could complete and serve my dishes in time. Dinner: Salmon filled bouche cases baked in a brisk oven, curried lamb; blackeye peas boiled with Creole rice, served piping hot in a moulded shape on a white plate; lettuce, cucumber, bell pepper and tomato salad with lime-juice enhanced French dressing; tropical fruit medley (fruit salad to you and me) with coconut-papaya cream accompaniment; fresh orangeade and mild clove-and-cinnamon tea to finish. Three hours. Lacking both money and opportunity to practise the menu it was a miracle I just whiskered in on the day.

My pride centred on the table arrangement as well. Mudsie's silver place setting and Grandad's silver napkin ring, treasures from their wealthier years, were polished to a fare-thee-well. They lay on Mudsie's best white machine embroidered, flour-bag tablecloth and napkin. Resembling linen of uneven weave, the flourbag tablecloth was given respectability by its edging of Irish lace, crocheted by Mummy. Laundered to white (ahem!)

perfection by Granny Adrianna, Oxley's launch had brought it to Georgetown with Mummy's last unbroken crystal bowl. Miss Mae lent her crystal vase and I stole a rose and freshly fallen rose petals from the grounds of Brickdam's Catholic Cathedral for the setting. Far from artistic I relied on the dramatic, designing the menu with pictures from travel agencies pasted on to good quality satin paper. As extra touches, the drinking glass, decorated with a slice of orange, was then chilled. The salad fork was also chilled and both were placed on the table just before serving, having added a frosting of sugar to the rim of the glass at the last minute. Completing the picture was the single rose bud, while Mummy's crystal bowl became the finger bowl in which swam pink and cream rose petals. Mudsie had seen these finger bowls in white homes where she had worked as a young servant. During the cooking, as the Nun examined that perfectly pressed, belted shirtwaist-dress, she looked past the mud splotches and merely said in my direction, "Oh. You're the one."

Talk of after-exam nerves! Flinging myself on the grass of the netball court outside the Home Ec room, face to the sun, white apron spread upwards covering me waist to head, I was beyond caring who saw me shaking. Others retired to the cloakroom for the discreet twenty minute sniffle. Bishops servants Dora and Winifred strode by and softly called me to them backstairs.

"Chile, weeping may tarry for de night but joy cometh in de morning. Dry yo eyes. Stand up straight. Carry yo self like all o' dem others. We proud yo even reach this far."

Home that evening.
"How you feel?"
"I don't know Miss Mae."
"How you think you do?"
"I think I passed, Miss Mae."
"Well, we gun see."

Later on.

"You do alright Mona?"

"I hope so Enid. Thanks."

"Well, everything outta your hands now."

"Yes. Enid. Thanks."

After listening with Keith to the late Radio Demerara news,
"You alright Bones?"

"Nah M'sieur."

"Why Bones?"

"Umm, I feel . . . I ent know . . . confused."

"'Bout what?"

"Dunno M'sieur."

"Look Donkey-face," he said, (I must admit I wore a loooong
face) "you can't even smile, eh? De exam's over, Stupidee!" We
broke up laughing.

"Stupidee m'backside! Wait till you sit next year, bow-legs!"

As he turned and shambled through the front door to wheel
our bicycles into the house for safety overnight, I gave a playful
kick to his bottom.

Like watchers for the deluge which breaks a year-long drought,
we kept our spirits buoyant through to results day in August.
Girls invited each other to house parties to meet their brothers
from Queen's College. I was asked to one party but had grown
out of all my going out clothes at this stage and had to decline.

Cycling home from Bookers in July one Saturday afternoon I
ran into a group of Upper Sixths outside the YWCA on
Brickdam. They were the pretties of Bishops and I often wished
I could join in their talk about boys. For example, everybody
drooled over a handsome devil called Chiquito. I had never even
seen him but felt I knew all about him from the spit press.

"What y'all doing?"

"Preparing the hall for a dance tonight. You coming?" they
asked. If pigs and tapirs flew first! With no party clothes nor

a date? My life of Bishops-ballet-and-Bookers rarely threw me together with available boys. The four males at ballet school had been promptly snaffled by the brown-skinned good lookers. The boys I had met through debating and elocution contests didn't relish girls who voiced strongly held opinions. Worse, I beat them more than a few times at debating, which won me prizes but no dates.

"I didn't know it was on. Nah. Can't come." That was true enough. I could have added, "Never had a date in my life. Know any bannahs?"

"Come and have a jump-up anyway," they urged.

"Couldn't get me hair pressed and styled by seven," I explained. I thought fleetingly of borrowing one of Enid's dresses. Stupid idea! I'd end up looking like a flat-chested sixteen, going on an ample bosom thirty, and boys might get the wrong impression. If only I had one pretty, teenage dress for best—a billowing skirt over two can-can petticoats and some flat dress shoes.

"Anyway what are your plans for the future?" we asked each other. Keane, a well admired pianist who played the hymns in assembly, would work in the Civil Service just a bit before going overseas.

"I'm off to Mona. Ha!" I'd heard the joke before. Lynette Smith-Green, local, short and personable, planned to study at the University College of the West Indies at Mona, Jamaica.

"And let me guess. You're off to England. University?" I offered.

"Too simple," the white sixth former with freckles laughed. "No challenge." This was matter of fact Maureen Birkett, who wasn't stuck up around us locals. Her British parents, white skin and clipped speech, suggested where she'd go. "Oxford?" I probed.

"Could be Bristol or St Andrews. You never know," Maureen teased.

"And you?"

"I looking for a lil' hold-on in the Civil Service if I get five O level passes." I couldn't aspire to their university heights.

"Why aren't you returning to Bishops?" Maureen was curious. "You could do Advanced levels and then attend university."

"Great! What would I do for money?" I chuckled, stating the obvious.

"You don't have to pay fees!"

"No? Enlighten me. You've met my fairy godmother? Or you want me to work obeah in a graveyard one ghost-night and win the Littlewoods Pool the next day! Win thousands o' pounds, eh Mo-Mo?" I joked.

"Just go and ask Miss Harris to extend your scholarship to the Upper Sixth. If you've five passes she must . . . er . . . should say yes." Maureen added cautiously.

"What'd'you mean?"

"Don't tell me! You don't know? Scholarship girls . . . their right to an extension . . ." Maureen said much more which didn't register. I smiled dumbstruck then waved goodbye and walked off, pushing my bicycle.

"Something wrong with your bike?" a voice sang out to my back.

"Nah," I flung over my shoulder, not daring to cycle home for fear of colliding excitedly into the back of a donkey-cart. Incredible. Absolutely. How was it possible for me to have attended Bishops five years without anyone telling me this? Another two years free! Did other scholarship girls know of the extension?

Monday afternoon Miss Taitt taught the beginners' class herself for the first time in months. A freshly laundered blouse was removed from my locker, shaking hands washed my oily face, styled my pressed hair, buffed my shoes, brushed my teeth and smoothed a borrowed tie into my skirt waist. I looked at my fingernails. A bit grubby and since it couldn't be helped, I brushed

143

them clean with my tooth brush. Then I went to beard the lion, Miss Harris, Molly-the-mop. Down the stairs and along the corridor my mind replayed the drama of my two memorable visits to her office.

I had gone in to argue for a place in a class that was difficult to get into, on the very first morning of the new school year, 1 September 1959.

"But, Miss Harris, I was told that girls'll be put into the Physics and Chem class if their Maths and Biology marks were good," I had begun.

She nodded but held her peace.

"Well Miss Harris, I've come to ask to be in that class."

"Those classes are filled to capacity already," she had said with finality in her voice.

"But Miss Harris I put my name down to do Physics and Chem at the end of last year and I haven't been chosen. But Eryl Evans was. And her marks in Maths and Bio weren't as good as mine. I came higher in both subjects than she did." I was trying to remain calm. So was Miss Harris.

"Eryl's parents want her to study medicine, so she has to take Physics and Chem." Miss Harris' voice was patient, her grey eyes watchful.

"My mother also told me she wants me to be a doctor, Miss Harris. So I have to take those subjects too," I countered.

"Well . . ." and there was a long pause while the wheels in our brains whirred and we both weighed the competing claims. The telephone rang distantly in the secretary's office next door. The beguiling fragrance of frangipani in a vase on her desk assailed my nose.

Eryl's family was Welsh, white, and well off. Her father, a brilliant scientist with a Queen's honour, was nationally respected and sat on the Board of Governors of Bishops. Eryl was a reasonable pupil, well behaved, attractive, clothes conscious and a bit of a snob. Eryl's marks were not as good as mine but then, who was I?

"Well, her name begins with E and yours with W. The class was full by the time the teachers came to your name," she said.

"Oh. So, were we chosen by our last names rather than by our marks?" my voice was a brittle, fake-Oxford Properly. The Mop folded her arms across her chest and let that pass.

"I'll put your name on a waiting list. If anyone drops out you'll be the first to get into the class," she offered.

"But Miss Harris, if someone drops out six weeks from now, who will teach me the beginnings of the subject. They're hard subjects even if I start with everyone now. I'll never catch up later on."

"That's the best I can offer," was her final remark.

"Miss Harris, I couldn't pay for extra lessons to catch up." No comment left her lips.

"I still can't see why I didn't get a place first, since my marks were better than hers." She showed me to the door. "Why can't someone get a place later if I drop out?" My voice was polite, soft, but too, too British. She had returned to her desk.

Two months or so later when Eryl dropped out I went back to Miss Harris.

"I can't take her place now. I'm too far behind . . . twenty four hours of lessons and weeks of homework. I should have been selected in the first place. On my marks rather than on my last name. I can't afford extra lessons to catch up, even if I could catch up." My voice held polite, quiet, refined fury. My face was respectful but unsmiling.

"I just knew she wouldn't stick with it. I would have." The Mop must have wondered why I'd come to her at all. Leaving the office I muttered just loudly enough for Molly to hear, "This school isn't fair to black pupils!"

Would that Parthian shot return to wound my cause now as the school year ended in July 1960?

145

I was now in her office promptly at 3.15 by her wall clock. "I should be able to support myself from my part-time jobs. And my behaviour has been good for the past two years." I presented my case standing, hands behind my back, spine ram rod straight, poised. I was bursting for a pee.

Molly seemed caught entirely off guard by my request.

"It really does depend on the number of passes you've secured. You need five. And . . . um . . . the level of your best three should be in the 70s," the Mop hedged. "So no decision can be made before the August results arrive from England." France! If only I'd known that I might go on to the sixths, I would've busted my backside in the exams. Certainly I'd scored seventyish in Bishops mock exams, but the real Oxford and Cambridge Joint Examinations Board Exam, competing with pupils from England itself, was quite a different matter. France! Now, just supposing I haven't the marks to gain a scholarship extension! I need parents to fight for me but where are they! I'd just have to pull something from up my sleeve.

"Would having a surname beginning with W count against me this time for getting into the class, please Miss Harris?" My voice sounded entirely innocent.

Her lips pursed, hands fumbled, weight shifted from one foot to the other and her arms came up to fold themselves tightly across her chest. She made a few false starts to speak, bit her lip but said nothing. The room temperature appeared to drop a good ten degrees while I observed some grey hairs on her chin then looked her in the eye. Molly was a long time and a few deep breaths replying.

"I wouldn't imagine so." The wall clock seemed to tick particularly loudly. I had been in here less than three minutes. My wide smile gave no hint of the terror I felt at tingling sweat rippling down my back. God, don't let me pee myself.

"Thank you very much, Miss Harris," my voice spilled cheerful enthusiasm and a hint of gratitude. "Good afternoon Miss Harris."

I walked quietly, gracefully, out of her office, past Miss Lall in the school's administration office, down the polished, wooden corridor and into the cloakroom where I sat on a toilet seat until I'd stopped shaking. Ballet could wait!

Thank the Almighty for stationery and stamps.

Dear Dad

. . . everyone with connections is snapping up Civil Service jobs. I'm not applying because I'm fairly confident that I'll have passed all six o levels, so I should be returning to Bishops in September. It'll look bad for a career too if I got a job then turned it down.

Bookers is a godsend but I'd love to win a Littlewoods Pool and have millions to spend on dental work and clothes. Even one good frock would be enough so I can go to parties . . . It was interesting to get all those postcards of your trip to Belgium, Paris and Holland. Can you speak French? I can. A little. And I have dreams! Like that ad: 'I dreamt I was in Paris in my Maidenform bra'. What an interesting life you must lead, visiting the Continent for holidays. I hope Miss Iris liked the trip too. Thanks for the letters and photos.

Awful about the Teddy Boys beating up West Indians in London. Why do they do it? Life in BG is a lot of politics too; rallies at Bourda Green and speeches about Dr Cheddi Jagan being a Communist. What's a Communist, Dad? Nobody says what it is, only that the government will jail you for being one. Thank heavens there's cricket! Have you ever seen Garfield Sobers, Rohan Khanai or Frank Worrel bat? That's my other dream . . . to see the West Indies play the MCC at Lords . . . Take care. Write soon.

Love,
Mona

Then we had a final Assembly in the hall; prizes awarded, house shields won and lost, cups proudly accepted by admirable prefects. We sang 'Lord dismiss us with thy blessing' and wished each other all the best. I willed myself to believe that this was not my final year at Bishops although I hadn't told my family about the possibility of another two years. I cried no tears. Accepted no goodbyes from the others. Breathed not a word to the other scholarship girls about extensions being available. I'd see them in the new school year. Or not.

A prompt reply from Wembley,

> Dear Mona,
>   . . . you said that you were sure you'd passed your exams. I hope when the results come out you'll have something to crow about. Perhaps you should take a leaf out of your sister's book. Claire writes such modest letters . . .

There was no money in the envelope either. I folded the paper, put it at the bottom of the suitcase which held my possessions, then promised myself to finish reading the other two pages of the letter when I felt less fragile. Maybe after results day. For now the Bookers holiday job had to keep my spirits buoyant. My supervisor, Bernie Periera, gave me tips on looking good on very little and on looking busy. 'You straighten the shoe boxes, polish the chrome store display stands and shine the glass cases whenever the big-boss, Mr Reyland, takes a turn through the ground floor'. She even taught me how to laugh.

Results came in the post from England after Keith had sailed home.

"Miss Mae!!Miss Mae!! I passed all six.!"

"Me chile, well done. Give God de praise!"

The appointment to see Miss Harris was set for my Bookers' lunch hour on Wednesday.

"So, Miss Harris, seeing that I've passed all six subjects . . ."

"Yes. You do seem to have three strong subjects. History, English and Biology . . . um . . . all over eighty percent." Barely over. The highest was 83.6 percent. Still, it topped the required marks. We were both silent. I was elated but on my mettle. What had been decided, dammit?

"Your behaviour was discussed with the staff. They are happy with your being made a prefect," Molly-the-mop was speaking deliberately, calmly dotting all the i's and crossing all the t's. I surmised that she was deciding as she went along whether to have back this pupil who argued over so many things.

"Surely she'll say 'Yes' now. I've got good marks," my mind was saying.

"Studies at Upper School level are altogether different. You may not be able to support yourself and carry three subjects as demanded by your scholarship regulations. That could also mean two years wasted, if you failed Advanced Level exams in '62 . . ." I could feel myself wanting to cry or scream.

"Miss Harris, with all due respect," I was glad I'd learnt that phrase debating, now keep the voice light and cheerful, "isn't that punishing me for being poor? I've done well in spite of being poor. I deserve to continue even though I am poor." No comment from the Mop. What else had I left to try?

I must swing this in my favour. Today. Lawd help me! What's this image in my mind's eye? That's it! Mimic that beguiling bull-dozer, Miss Taitt. Bulb-bright. On went my ballet smile. The back grew straight. I dropped my shoulders. One hand grasped the wrist of the other in front of me, as Royalty do. I stood motionless. How could Molly look at this and still turn me down?

"That seems to be all. So. Umm. Very well. Then . . . we shall see. In September." I kept the smile firmly in place. Kept the pressure on. Stood. Silently. Smiling. "We'll . . . umm . . . er, expect you then," she added.

I wasn't blessed well coming back in September for her to 'see' what she would do then. So I chose to interpret her words to suit myself.

"Thank you very much Miss Harris. I'll do my best in the new school year as a sixth former. I'll study hard. And I'll try to be a good prefect. My thanks for being able to return, Miss Harris. Many thanks." Then I was gone.

149

"Dora," I called at the door to the back stairs' quarters, "Y'all will see me for another two years."

"Chile, what we told you? God don't wear pyjamas. He don't slumber nor sleep! Could you come in here and show me how to arrange dese flowers den?"

Inside as we pretended to poke sprigs of bougainvillaea this way and that Dora whispered, "Eh, Eh! I surprise dey let you back in!"

"Why?" I whispered.

"Dey said you was mixed up in some politics."

"Me?" Incredible.

"You! They was talking say, you was demonstrating 'gainst de government."

"Me Dora?" I managed, stunned. "I don't go to no rallies."

"You was in front o' de Treasury?" Dora insisted.

"O Lawd!" I said, feeling as if kicked in my tail bone. "Why people does say things that ent really true?"

"You didn't do it then?" Dora asked in a fierce whisper.

"No. It wasn't 'gainst the government. It was for my religion."

"So you was in de politics den!"

"No. It was m'religion. Not politics." I corrected.

"Is what's you religion?"

"Um . . ."

"De Coptic Church?" Dora pressed.

"No."

"You is a Jordan Knight?" she tried again.

"No." Then I was silent.

"Y'all does dress up in white? Well . . ." Dora probed, but as I volunteered nothing she added, "All I know is dat de government don't want fo let you back in. De High Up People . . . But go with God, chile. And careful, y'hear?"

"Thanks Dora," I said, finally understanding The Mop's hesitation.

"You arrange dese flowers nice for me. Thanks," she sang

150

out to my disappearing back just in case we had been observed. Then I ran to my cycle, heart pounding, and bike-sprinted to Bookers.

Seventeen

The beat of the launch engine was reassuring but sleep evaded me on the trip home. Who could have told me that my beloved brown Demerara would one day fail to excite me? The memory of Miss Mae's face, engagingly mobile as a saki-winki monkey's when she heard the news, that was a delightfully memorable gift. The scene danced before my eyes.

"Praise God, chile." Miss Mae was stuffing rice and coconut milk into animal entrails, creating coils of white pudding sausages. She sold the delicacy in the evenings to make a few shillings.

"Can I continue here for another two years?" You wouldn't have guessed that I was fearful of the reply.

"Why not?" her tone was encouraging.

"Same amount for board? Twenty-five dollars a month?" I was at her mercy.

"Same amount."

"Thanks Miss Mae." The tension left me. My smile was heartfelt.

"Is all right." Shy Miss Mae was never one for florid speeches.

"Well. You done well. First in yo' family to get High School certificate." Her smile was magical, revealing well made false teeth.

"Nah," I corrected. "All o' we did this. This is me family's certificate." Then I could say no more, in Creolese or Properly. Nor was this an attempt at modesty. I spoke the unvarnished truth.

Enid said a brief "Well done". Her mind was on sewing a customer's ruched, orange, voile-over-taffeta dress for Saturday's races.

I could afford only two days from Bookers to go home. "I showed them!" Mummy exulted when she heard the news the instant we'd got past the shop counter. She clapped, pulled her skirt way up her thighs, shook her hips, laughed, danced to a calypso she shouted, stomped and hollered at the news. It was as well the breadshop had no customers.

"I said I'll educate my children and by heavens I have! They couldn't stop me. I walked without shoes! With holes in my underwear! My stomach rumbling for food! But God heard my cry. I say 'Take that!' to my blasted headmaster and to all the rest o' them!" and Mummy babbled psalms and screamed and zegged all by herself, as I had done at Wakenaam. Although I didn't see things quite by her lights this was a time for celebrations, not for arguments.

"No. I don't want a special meal. No presents neither. All I want is everyone here for dinner. I travelled a whole day for this hour. And I don't want Shalto coming in to bless anything." My clearly stated wishes were well understood.

Generations of women busied themselves with cutlery, a tablecloth and glasses; cassava, breadfruit, plantain and codfish. Coconut milk, cornmeal dumplings and peppers were added to cook an African metagee. As the meal simmered, Granny Adrianna, who was living again at Mudsie's, cried at the news. Sitting in the kitchen-dining area behind the bread shop, she began her favourite Psalm, 103.

"Bless the Lord, O my soul, and all that is within me bless His Holy name . . ." I joined her, reciting the Psalm of Thanks by heart.

"Which Psalm yo wants us to say now?" Granny invited my choice as we prayed. This was a first, praying as equals.

"Psalm 91. My favourite," I replied, and we intoned together.

"He that dwelleth in the secret place of the most High shall abide under the shadow of the Almighty . . ." Then we sang in unison 'The Gloria' in Latin and my anthem, 'Thanks be to God'. When Granny Adrianna said one of her prayers which you'd think would never end, for the first time I didn't mock her tears. As her black, boney, arthritic hands sat atop my woolly head to bless me I experienced a feeling of awe I had never known before. It seemed as though thousands of ancestral presences, of slaves long dead who had hoped for such a moment as this, were blessing me, their descendant. This was not my triumph but the triumph of our people who'd hoped against all odds. A people who had died in appalling circumstances after living brutish lives. A people who had taught us never to give up. Certainly we had to live secretly, shrewdly, silently, but even when we could not reveal our hatred of ill treatment, of injustice, we were always to refuse to agree with it. The world moved back and forth around us, women busily selling bread, cooking and table setting, while we sat lost in a cocoon of unity. We talked softly of the times at the secret farm and at Khailan's flat in Georgetown. She asked me if I had a boy-friend and found it odd that I hadn't one at my age. Mysteriously, I felt myself the spiritual daughter of Old Granny Adrianna.

"Not bad, Boney Yard. Congrats you skinny assed picknee," Keith tough-talked but hugged me gently. "So. We're together. At Miss Mae. Another year. At least." His fifteen year old body was filling out at the chest. He was getting fuzz on his chin, was taller than me now and . . . was his voice fog-horn deep!

"Haul you bow-legged backside!" I joshed back.

"You not as stupidee as you look, eh donkey-face?" That from Keith was high praise.

"Kiss me ass."

"Mummy, y'hear how Boney-Yard cussing now she got the cer-fit-ecate? What sort o' Bishop girl is dat?"

154

"Y'all behave y'self!" Mudsie warned now that customers were in the shop.

We hooted and screamed at nothing. Then when he wasn't looking I gave him a playful slap on the side of his head and fell over laughing.

Claire wasn't at home to share the moment, but Mudsie said, "Remember to tell God 'Thanks'," and proceeded to boast to the customers who came in. "Well, me grandpicknee just passed she GEC. Six subjects. Going forward at Bishops for another two more years. Well, the good Lord got a hand in everything, nuh? Give God the praise."

"Eh? Eh? Congratulations Miz Nelson," they'd say.

"Thank you me chile," Mudsie would croon. Often they'd add, "Little Miz Nelson, just continue to study yo books. Don't bother with no boyfriend-story. Boys is a worry. Books before boys nuh?" Silence was always the wisest response. When they'd left, "Its GCE Mudsie. General Certificate of Education," I'd say by way of correction, but who cared?

Grandad made a speech during dinner that night. I noticed his old-blue eyes, perfect teeth and left handed dexterity. He was interrupted by Mudsie's having to get up to sell bananas, cheese, pies and cigarettes to customers. It felt like listening to the oration of a very proper, unfamiliar visitor. He spoke like the white Canadians at the hospital. We didn't do things this way! Grandad and I had no common memories, no joys or pains, no songs or arguments. He'd shared neither his time nor his money with the family these past forty years as Mackenzie Hospital's chief pharmacist. He'd chosen to live across the river at Mackenzie. In the hospital compound, in a white people house the company had provided him rent free. He'd spent his wealth on women. Now, retired and returned to our side of the river to live in the house that Mudsie alone had built, we were trying to include this stranger. Making him welcome in a tight circle of capable

155

mothers. No matter. I left the table richer than I had come to it, because of everyone's presence.

Yet, I was not entirely at one with the spirit of the celebrations. I valued the certificate because it promised me work in the Civil Service, and a good wage. But I did not think that being a Bishops girl made me a finer person. I valued 'De White People's knowledge' but it had cost me more than money and effort. It had required me to despise my blackness, my people and my country. Arriving at Bishops in 1955, rich in self-confidence and self-love, I had gained a canoe full of conflicts, confusion over what things I should value, and a good deal of self-loathing. Yet I couldn't discuss any of this with my family. Tonight they'd felt joy and triumph. I knew they wouldn't understand if I'd said that their dream had been my nightmare.

"And will I see you in the new academic year?" Miss Taitt was asking the night before school resumed in September 1960.

"If I may, Miss Taitt. I'm looking forward to dancing for another year. Maybe, for life." If I were frank I would have put it baldly saying "I need this job to pay my board!". While I suspected that Miss Taitt was not taken in for a minute, she did prefer civilised conversation.

"Will you get past the riots, the demonstrations, the troops, safely?" The perturbed look contradicted her composed stance.

"Miss Taitt, I've been working in Water Street all August. Never had trouble. You just have to make sure you're not stupid. That you don't shout, 'WE WANT INDEPENDENCE!'. The ones they're arresting shout, 'P.P.P.', you know, Dr Jagan's People's Progressive Party. Or they show three fingers to the police. Police don't even need an excuse like that to dash them inside the Black Maria." I was forgetting myself, putting things crudely. I retreated into a quiet tone. "I'll be safe, Miss Taitt."

"The political situation . . ." she trailed off.

"I know," I said. "My grandmother can't get Manitoba Maid

156

wheatflour from Canada because of the strikes. So, her bread business is going under . . . fewer customers." And out of nowhere sprang the tears.

"You have a minute?" Miss Taitt asked. I nodded. "Why not step inside?"

We sat at the magnificently polished dining table in the vast dining salon while Miss Taitt brought me tea in an ornate, silver teapot, on a silver tray with wafer-thin Royal Doulton porcelain tea cups and saucers. A china cake stand held miniature almond biscuits, made with a lot finer sugar and more butter than Mudsie's commercial version. Blanched almonds were pressed into the tops.

"Well, I'm hoping you'll consider joining the company for rehearsals. This year we'll go until 9 p.m." I was learning to smile and say little with Miss Taitt, so I stirred my tea.

"I'll tell you why. History and Culture Week celebrations. I've a Guianese Legend in mind for the Queen's College stage. Amalivaka. About the Amerindian god who came riding out of the sun in his dug-out canoe after the Great Flood. I've begun writing the music." I still said nothing. "If your studies permit," she added.

"If my studies permit, Miss Taitt. Bishops, er, invited me . . . um . . . took me back, but . . ." It would have been unwise to have said more.

"Of course. I see," she said.

"Thank you then, Miss Taitt," my words caressed the air as lightly and quietly as a humming bird's wings. I had been invited to join the Ballet Guiana Dance Company!

There were no dazzling bonfires shooting sparks in my eyes or soaring leaps of my heart this time. No fouetté turns of joy at the invitation to do company rehearsals after teaching a beginners' class. I foresaw only grinding hard work, awfully low pay, struggles for study time and perpetual tiredness. And where was the leisure time to party and meet Queen's College boys?

157

To learn to date and rock-n'-roll? But . . . this was the price of ballet and Bishops. We sat in companionable silence a long time; my thoughts lost in the wonder of ballet on my life. It had made so much possible. And rendered so much impossible!

"What was studying ballet like in New York, Miss Taitt?" Could it have been comparable to those exquisite Royal Ballet accounts of the lives of Margot Fonteyn or of Ninette de Valois, I wondered.

"It was difficult getting into a decent school because I'm coloured." She used the old fashioned 'coloured'. "And even when I was clearly superior to most of the others, the best jobs given me were in the back row of the corps de ballet where I was fair-skinned enough to be mistaken for a white dancer by the audience." Words failed me. This happened to fair skinned Miss Taitt!

"Truly. Years, years of classes in studios so cold in the winter, I cried while I did pliés. My fingers cracked. They bled when I bent them to grip the barre. The way you've done it, I did it. Spent months sneaking into company rehearsals. Learning the routines from behind the curtains in the wings. Caught between getting producers to see how good I was, and being invisible so I could learn the dances, even though they wouldn't let me into a company." She was staring absently at the rim of her teacup.

"Years of living on little, typing to pay the rent, practising every evening and long into the nights. Lonely for BG. For family. I even missed my mother's funeral, home, here. And what was the prize? The reward? Nothing for a coloured dancer. So, I gave up New York and came home to share my knowledge with my own people."

As always Miss Taitt, when she became conscious of herself again, smiled her bright dancer's smile which masked unmentionable memories. I returned her smile, feeling suddenly unable to breathe. I thanked her softly for the tea and rode away home trembling with despair and desperate hope for my dancing future. Miss Taitt's fate could be mine. Yet, mightn't fate treat me more kindly than it had my teacher and my ancestors? My job was to hope; hope against the reality before my eyes.

Eighteen

I felt the calm equal of every other Sixth Former when I entered the Bishops gate in September 1960. The white cotton school blouse, green uniform skirt, white socks, brown leather shoes, tie, hat and hat band had all been paid for with my own Bookers' wages. A new, reliable, zippered bag bulged with my own second-hand text books. With the care of an accountant a tiny sum remaining from my holiday pay might cover shoe polish, toiletries, laundry soap, stamps and stationery. Urgent dental work was beyond my means. The Victoria House mistress presented me with a silver prefect's badge which I pinned to my chest. I felt unhappy having the authority it invited me to exercise.

"But, I'll cross that bridge when I come to it," I promised myself.

"I want to mark my O level success and my seventeenth year with something precious," I told myself a good ten weeks past my birthday. Last year's sixteenth birthday had been remembered only at 8 p.m. when shaking, sweaty hands untied the pink ribbons of my ballet slippers. No family member had remembered or sent a card either. Utterly exhausted I'd hardly known how empty I'd felt in that moment, slumped in the ballet school's dressing room.

"Sweet Sixteen and never been kissed. Wouldn't mind either!" I'd laughed at myself.

"If only I were as pretty as Claire. And always said whatever was nice. And didn't argue about anything. And wore clothes like Enid. And came from a family like Sandra Williams," I'd daydreamed cycling home in 1959.

Now, a year later . . . Hell! I must dig up my father's letter and read the two pages I never bothered to finish. Then I'll write and apologise for the two months' delay. Must pen a long, sweet, modest letter. I'll discuss politics — he talks about that a lot. And cricket. And Princess Margaret. And the wonderful, year-long summer weather in BG. And I'll mention my return to Bishops in the most casual manner in exactly five words in the final sentence. "Incidentally, I'm continuing at Bishops." Wasn't it one of my English mistresses who told us "Girls, hypocrisy pays homage to virtue." I must remember that.

Scraping together all I could afford, five dollars, in late September 1960 I spent a lunch hour mesmerised by trays of gold and silver. Pendants, lockets, brooches and tie-clips, fob watches, noserings, which were worn by some East Indian women, earrings, wrist and ankle bracelets, watch straps, necklaces and finger rings. I made my modest purchase. Turning to leave the pawn shop I playfully pushed the door of one of its pawning cubicles. At the sight and touch of the slatted door a familiar memory began to surface.

Emerging from the Portuguese Pawn Brokery into the heat and blinding midday light I carried a box stuffed with cotton wool. In it nestled a ring of Guiana gold. Striding across a few streets to the shade of a flamboyant tree my mind meandered back. Past Miss Mae, Olivia, Granny Adrianna, Danny Boy, Uncle Hulbert; home with Mudsie, with Aunt Lydia Maud and Aunt Carrie. I'm at Mudsie's two-storied house at Christianburg.

No, I'm not attending school. I am nearly four years old. Mummy stands me up against the slatted door of Mudsie's bedroom on the upper storey. She moves her face close, in front of my nose.

"Say what I tell you," she directs me. "Say, I-will-go-to-Bishops!" The words are teased out deliberately.

"I gun go to Bishops." I parrot imperfectly in Creolese.

Now I ride knowingly on this ambitious, turbulent water-way, shooting rapids, dodging eddies, paddling dexterously in the grip of swift currents, determined to stay afloat.

Under the flamboyant tree, celebrating my return to Bishops and my being seventeen, I'm conscious of the blinding, scorching midday heat. There's a smelly drainage canal beside me.

I have no words for this moment. No songs, no dances, no shouts, no speeches, psalms or poems from relatives. No feast. No Passover firelight adorns this calm, private instant in a buffeted life. I lift out and place the delicate, tiny, gold ring carefully on the smallest finger of my right hand. Then, I stuff the box into my uniform skirt pocket, jump on my bike and zoom to school. Past Alphonso's record store I speed round St George's Cathedral, up to the gate in the white picket fence and dismount in time for the afternoon classes at Bishops.

"Lawd, Ah ready!" I say.